FROM CLICKS TO CONVERSIONS:

The Tactical Guide to Organic Search Marketing

ERIC BONNEMAN AND JACK BONNEMAN

From Clicks to Conversions:
The Tactical Guide to Organic Search Marketing

First Edition: December, 2024
ISBN: 979-8-218-58310-1
Printed in the United States of America.

For inquiries or bulk orders, contact:
www.thekingofsearch.com

Table of Contents

Conversion Focused, Authority-Building, Organic Search Marketing

Welcome to **From Clicks to Conversions: The Tactical Guide to Organic Search Marketing**, a comprehensive journey into the heart of modern SEO and content creation strategies.

Our approach is not just theory; it's a distilled working framework honed from years of experience and success. We understand the constantly evolving nature of search engines and consumer behavior. Thus, we've crafted a strategy that adapts to these changes while maintaining a solid foundation in the core principles of SEO and content marketing. We aim to transition you from traditional models to a more dynamic, integrated approach.

This book is more than a guide; it's a blueprint for those looking to dominate search engines through thoughtful, strategic content creation and optimization. Whether you're looking to break through with cutting-edge techniques or refine your existing strategies to align with the current search marketing landscape, we'll show you how to create a cohesive and powerful online presence that attracts, retains, and converts your target audience.

This is the same powerful framework we use at The King of Search, where we're committed to conversion-focused, authority-building organic search marketing. For additional resources and support, or to see how these strategies work in real time, visit us at thekingofsearch.com/the-lab/.

Chapter 1:
The Framework

When discussing search marketing, we must examine the interplay between the website, search optimization, content creation, analytics, and CRO (Conversion Rate Optimization). When you look at these areas as a cohesive unit, they form an unbeatable strategy.

Search marketing is the strategic promotion of a website by increasing its visibility in search engine results pages (SERPs) through paid and unpaid efforts.

Search marketing is not static; it's a field in constant flux. Since the inception of the internet, the landscape has undergone several significant shifts. Sophisticated algorithms like Google's Panda and Penguin changed the game, penalizing poor-quality content and black-hat SEO (Search Engine Optimization) techniques. The proliferation of mobile browsing, voice search, and local search optimization have further expanded the domain of search marketing. Understanding user behavior and preferences is now more critical than ever.

But this evolution isn't just technological. It's also about perception, how people see search marketing. Over the years, it has transformed from a "nice-to-have" to a "must-have" in a business's arsenal.

Search marketing is about visibility, but it's also about credibility. When a site ranks high, it isn't just seen – it's perceived as authoritative and trustworthy. It's the difference between being a known entity in an industry or remaining obscured by competitors.

With data analytics, we can track user behavior, understand what they seek, how they navigate, and what turns their interest into action. This wealth of data enables businesses to create highly targeted, relevant content and advertisements, making every marketing dollar count.

Search marketing is a complex, evolving discipline that requires a deep understanding of technology, psychology, and business strategy. It's no longer just about "getting found" online. It's about building a complete online presence that resonates with the target audience, aligns with search engine algorithms, and drives measurable outcomes.

For those new to the world of organic search marketing, this book may seem complex, and it is to a degree. But, if you've ever gone down the thousands of SEO and search marketing rabbit holes you find during a Google search about the topic, you'll soon find we have weeded out 99% of that and left you with precisely what you need to understand and excel at to make it in search.

This guide is the culmination of years upon years of sifting through methodologies, implementation, testing, and reiteration - distilled into one specific framework that works every time.

The Website

To truly resonate with an ideal client base and meet your business goals, the site needs to be a finely tuned machine designed to attract, engage, and convert the target audience. This process shouldn't be a scattergun approach.

It demands a deliberate strategy in design and content that fulfills a specific need.

The website is there to lead ideal clients through a journey from initial curiosity to the ultimate decision to engage with the business. To do this effectively, the website must be highly targeted. This means understanding the psyche of the ideal client—what drives them, what challenges they face, and what solutions they're seeking. Accordingly, the website should offer content that addresses the varying stages of your visitors' decision-making journey. For those on the brink of decision, the route to action should be unmistakable—free from unnecessary barriers, providing a direct path to what you want them to do.

But let's not forget about the seekers—the ones who need a deeper understanding before they make a move. For these visitors, the website should offer expanded explanations, detailed case studies, insightful articles, and FAQs that anticipate their questions and concerns.

This content shouldn't be tucked away in obscure corners of the site, either. It needs to be interlinked logically, allowing visitors to navigate effortlessly from general information to the nitty-gritty details, all while keeping that ultimate conversion goal in sight.

And let's talk about UX (User Experience) for a second. The website must be intuitive, with a clean design that makes navigation a breeze. This isn't just aesthetic; it's about functionality and driving conversions. The site's structure should guide visitors through a logical flow, from initial interest to deeper exploration and conversion. Every element, from the layout to the call-to-action, should be designed with the ideal client in mind.

The website should serve as a comprehensive platform that meets the target audience's immediate needs and offers them a reason to stay, explore, and ultimately commit. It's a balance between simplicity and depth, between attraction and conversion. Get this foundation right, and you've set the stage for a search marketing campaign that doesn't just drive traffic but also converts traffic.

The website is not just a first impression; it's the best tool for building lasting relationships. Make it a place where these ideal clients feel understood, informed, and inspired to take action.

Writing Content

Content writing is the art and science of producing text that informs, engages, and inspires action. It is about understanding the power of words and using them to create a tangible impact on the targeted clients or consumers.

Writing demands clarity, conciseness, and relevance. Every sentence must serve a purpose, whether it's to educate, persuade, or entertain. The writer's task is to distill complex ideas into accessible and engaging prose, guiding readers through a narrative that aligns with their needs and interests. A well-crafted piece of content speaks directly to the reader, making them feel seen and understood.

Precision is key in content writing. Just as a PPC (Pay-Per-Click) campaign targets specific keywords, content writing involves careful language selection to resonate with targeted demographics. It's a balance of creativity and strategy, ensuring that every word contributes to the campaign's overall goal.

Effective content writing is also about storytelling. It's not just presenting facts or information; it's about weaving these elements into a narrative that captivates the reader and leads them along the desired path.

Content Marketing

Content guides potential customers through their journey from initial research to the final act of conversion. There's a balance between providing the right information at the right time, establishing authority, and subtly steering the journey toward a conversion action.

Content marketing is not a one-size-fits-all solution. It is inherently nuanced and dynamic, adapting and evolving as potential customers traverse their decision-making process.

We segment this decision-making process into three simple stages:

1. Initial Research
2. Consideration
3. Final Conversion

Understanding and catering to the needs of potential customers at each of these stages is the key to effectively nurturing leads and guiding them toward making a well-informed decision.

In the Research phase, potential customers are on a quest for information. They are not yet ready to purchase; their journey is driven by the mission to understand their needs or challenges better. At this stage, content marketing efforts should be focused on providing knowledge and insight. The aim is to offer content that is not just captivating but rich in substance, laying a foundation of trust and establishing the brand as an authoritative figure in the field.

As these leads progress into the consideration phase, their journey moves to evaluating potential solutions. The content must evolve in tandem, shifting from purely informational to more solution-centric. This phase is about showcasing knowledge and the practical application and effectiveness of the solutions offered, further solidifying the brand's position as a trustworthy and competent advisor.

The final push, the Conversion phase, is where the strategy peaks. Conversion stage content will function best after establishing credibility and trust built through the preceding content. The content at this stage is built around precision strikes. Content here should be laser-focused and geared towards conversion actions.

This entire journey is about being in tune with the audience's shifting needs and mindsets, providing content that addresses their current queries and anticipates and addresses future ones. This process ensures that the brand is not merely a bystander in the customer's decision-making process but an influence all along the way.

Content Distribution

Content is only half the battle. The other half? Make sure it gets in front of eyeballs. And not just any eyeballs, but the right ones.

When you consistently create high-quality, relevant content, search engines will rank the site for it. While content marketing works its organic magic in the background, distribution methods step in to supercharge its reach.

Distribution channels—social media, email marketing, syndication, or paid ads—act as amplifiers, projecting your voice further and broader. It's about tapping into existing communities, leveraging platforms where the target audience already spends their time, and delivering content directly to them.

This dual strategy, organic + distribution, ensures that while playing the long game with the benefits of organic, you're also making strategic, immediate inroads into the target audience's world through on-point distribution. It's not an either/or scenario; it's a powerful combination that maximizes exposure, engagement, and, ultimately, the impact of your marketing efforts.

Remember, the goal of content distribution is not just to throw your content into the ether and hope for the best. It's about strategically placing your content where the audience is, engaging them meaningfully, and bringing them back to the site.

Analytics

The key to surviving and thriving in search lies in the gold mine of insights: analytics data. It's what transforms guesswork into precision-targeted strategies, allowing you to understand not just what's happening but why it's happening and how you can pivot for better results.

At the heart of analytics lies its power to track and optimize every facet of your search marketing campaign. From the moment a visitor lands on a website, every click, every scroll, and every interaction is a goldmine of information.

But the true artistry in analytics is not merely in gathering this data; it's in interpreting it to understand the story it tells about the audience and your strategy's performance. When launching a content marketing campaign, analytics allows you to monitor which pieces of content are resonating with the audience, providing the answers to questions like:

– Are they engaging more with long-form or short-form content?
– Which topics are they gravitating towards?
– How much time are users spending on each piece of content?
– What is the click-through rate from your content to other parts of your website?
– Which content is driving actual conversions?
– Are visitors who read a specific article more likely to click on your call-to-action?

This level of insight is invaluable for fine-tuning your content strategy alongside every other component of your marketing efforts.

Perhaps the most transformative aspect is its ability to elucidate the customer journey. Every customer's path to purchase is a unique narrative filled with distinct touch-points and interactions. Analytics lets you map this journey, providing insights into customer behavior, preferences, and pain points. This knowledge is instrumental in creating a marketing strategy that meets and anticipates customer needs, ensuring the brand is always one step ahead.

In search marketing, where data is king, understanding and leveraging analytics separates those who are merely participating from those leading it, pushing boundaries, and redefining what it means to truly dominate in search.

Conversion Rate Optimization

Conversion Rate Optimization (CRO) is the process of enhancing a website and its content to increase conversions - a process where science meets creativity and analytics shakes hands with user experience.

CRO is more than just a tactic; it's a mindset. It's the relentless pursuit of ensuring every aspect of a business presence is aligned with its ultimate goal: maximizing return on investment (ROI). Every detail matters. Whether tweaking a landing page, refining a call-to-action (CTA), or streamlining the checkout process, every element is an opportunity to increase conversions.

CRO is about understanding the subtleties of user behavior. It's about getting into the audience's psyche, discovering what makes them click and prompts them to act. It's not making arbitrary changes; it's making informed, data-driven decisions.

This understanding is then translated into tangible changes on the website and in the marketing campaigns as a whole. From simplifying user flow to maximizing CTA placement, each adjustment is a step towards perfecting the user's journey from a visitor to a customer.

Integrating these tactics into your overall strategy isn't about incremental improvements; it's about leaps in conversion performance. CRO is an art form where precision meets intuition, and data informs creativity. It's an element that tightens the screws and oils the gears of your digital machine, ensuring it runs smoothly and efficiently.

Cohesion

Merging different search marketing strategies goes beyond just mixing various actions. It's about creating a unified effort where each part is precisely tuned to boost overall performance. Each technique—from content creation and targeted distribution to the meticulous use of analytics and CRO—is carefully chosen for each role in a more extensive, unified campaign.

This convergence of strategies isn't just about doing "everything." It's about doing the right things in the right way, at the right time, for maximum effect. Every tactic has its place, yet all aim towards a common goal: to stand out in the market and convert engagement into tangible results.

With this coordinated approach, we don't just pile techniques on each other; we build an integrated, synchronized campaign striving for greater visibility and effectiveness.

Chapter 2:
The Website

Everything in this book, every tactic, tool, and instruction - starts with the website you're working on.

A well-designed website doesn't just look good; it facilitates user interaction and provides intuittive navigation, quick access to information, and an engaging overall experience.

Web design may not be our primary focus when it comes to being a search marketer, but it's an area of knowledge we can't afford to neglect.

In our agency, we prioritize the assessment of these foundational website elements. If a website falls short of meeting these fundamental standards, we often refer the client to a trusted web design partner to address these issues before proceeding further.

That conversation goes something like this:

"Hello, thank you for reaching out to The King of Search. I'm Eric, and I've had a chance to review your industry and your offerings. I believe your project aligns perfectly with our expertise. However, after looking at your website, it's clear that it needs quite a bit of work – a complete redesign on a new platform. We want to ensure that we can deliver the best results, and that requires a solid foundation.

In this case, I'd recommend having a conversation with our trusted web design partner, Clay, over at Steamworks. They specialize in creating brand-focused, converting websites that align with our optimization strategies. If you decide to move forward with them and get your website redesigned, we can step in just before the launch to ensure everything is set up for success right from the start."

Client: "That sounds reasonable. I'll get in touch with Clay and see what we can work out."

This approach saves everyone from potential headaches and ensures a smoother journey towards achieving their goals.

There's also a unique opportunity for web designers to expand their skill set by delving into search marketing. Understanding the core requirements of a website from a search marketer's perspective, seamlessly integrating these needs during the website's construction, and delivering a *ready-to-market* product will set you apart from the vast majority of designers in the field today.

The Impact of Web Design

Websites are living, breathing representations of businesses and brands at the core of the user experience. A website is open 24/7 and is accessible to potential customers from around the world. It's where brands meet their audience—and the quality of this meeting can make all the difference for the business.

When visitors land on a website, they make lightning-fast evaluations of its appearance and functionality. An outdated or cluttered design can deter users, leading to high bounce rates (fast exits). Conversely, an appealing and well-organized layout can immediately captivate visitors and keep them exploring—enticing them to dive deeper into what you offer.

Website optimization isn't solely about impressing algorithms; it's also about providing a superior experience for human visitors. It's about creating an online environment where users effortlessly *find* what they seek, *trust* the information they discover, and *feel* compelled to take action.

Key Elements of a Well-Designed Website

Think of these elements as the building blocks to an effective strategy—each one uniquely crafting an experience that leaves visitors impressed and genuinely engaged.

A well-designed website seamlessly combines form and function, ensuring every click, scroll, and interaction serves a purpose.

Responsive Design

Responsive design ensures the website functions seamlessly across various devices, from desktops to smartphones to tablets.

I'll keep this part short, as it should be the norm by now, but...

Mobile optimization is a necessity.

It feels ridiculous to still be explaining this today, but we continue to run into sites that have yet to create a mobile-friendly user experience.

For those who have yet to go mobile, consider these facts:

- **Mobile** Users Are Everywhere: Billions of people access the internet through mobile devices. Ignoring this massive user base means missing out on most potential customers. Across various industries, mobile visits typically make up between 65% and 85% of daily traffic.

- **Improved User Experience**: Mobile users expect a smooth and enjoyable browsing experience. Responsive design ensures the website looks great and functions well on smaller screens, enhancing user interaction.
- **Search Engine Ranking**: Google and other search engines have long prioritized mobile-friendly websites in their rankings. Responsive design positively impacts a website's search engine visibility.

Responsive design is a design approach where the website adapts to the screen size and resolution of the device used to access it.

This is done through fluid grids that automatically adjust the layout and proportions of page elements based on the screen width, ensuring that content remains readable.

- Images are scaled and optimized to fit the screen, preventing users from needing to zoom in or out. This maintains image quality, optimizes page performance, and, most importantly, enhances user experience.
- Cascading Style Sheets (CSS) media queries apply different styles and layouts based on screen size. This allows for the creation of mobile-friendly navigation menus, fonts, and spacing.
- Creating a responsive design is the first step. Thorough testing will help ensure a flawless user experience on various devices.

Use online testing tools and screen emulators to view the website on different devices, screen sizes, and aspect ratios. As new devices and screen sizes emerge, periodically review and update the responsive design to maintain effectiveness.

- Tools like Google's Mobile-Friendly Test (Lighthouse inside of Chrome DevTools) can provide insights into mobile optimization.

- Test the responsive design across multiple web browsers to ensure compatibility and consistency.

- Conduct user testing with individuals who use different devices. Gather feedback and make necessary adjustments based on their experiences.

By prioritizing responsive design, you enhance user experience, meet today's most basic demands, and improve conversion performance.

Visual Appeal

Visuals grab attention instantly—they're the first thing visitors will notice on a website. They include everything from the layout and color scheme to fonts and images. These elements work together to create an immediate impression.

Some research has shown that it takes only about 50 milliseconds for users to form that initial impression.[1] This split-second judgment can influence whether they stay, explore, or click away. Thus, visual elements are some of the most powerful tools in your arsenal for conveying a brand's personality and values. They help establish trust and credibility with the target audience.

Color, typography, and imagery are the creative tools that web designers employ to shape this experience, and their mastery can profoundly influence how users perceive the brand and interact with content.

---

[1] Lindgaard, G., Fernandes, G., Dudek, C., & Brown, J. (2006). Attention web designers: You have 50 milliseconds to make a good first impression! Behaviour & Information Technology, 25(2), 115-126.

Color

Don't just pick colors—deploy them. Choose a color scheme that aligns with the brand and resonates with the target audience.

Consider the psychology of colors. Different colors can evoke various emotions and associations. Use color strategically to guide users' attention and create a cohesive visual experience.

Typography

Typography refers to the fonts used on a website. You can think of it as the brand's voice in visual form. So, select fonts that are easy to read and align with the brand's tone.

Combining a readable body font and a distinctive headline font can add personality to the design. Think of typography as a subtle yet powerful influencer in user experience and brand messaging.

Imagery

High-quality images and graphics can significantly enhance the website's visual appeal.

With images come speed concerns. Speed is a silent player in user experience, often overlooked but always critical. Users are less likely to engage with a site that takes too long to load. Optimize images and visual elements to prevent slow loading times. This can be solved by deploying fast-loading file formats. JPG and PNG file types can be compressed, while WebP provides the best overall performance.

Alongside this, correctly resize the images as appropriate for their application. If you're putting an image in a 300x300px element, the image should be resized to 300x300px at the file level.

While visual appeal is important, it should never come at the expense of user experience. Every design choice, from imagery to layout, should ultimately enhance and stream-line the user's journey toward the desired action.

Integrated CTAs

CTAs are not just buttons or links; they are the tactical maneuvers guiding visitors toward decisive actions.

These actions can vary widely depending on the website's goals, but common CTAs include:

- Making a purchase
- Signing up for a newsletter
- Requesting a quote
- Downloading a resource
- Contacting the business

Effective CTAs require thoughtful placement and design. They should be highly visible and immediately distinguish-able from other page elements. Use contrasting colors, bold typography, or buttons to make them stand out.

CTAs should be strategically placed where users are most likely to notice them. Common locations include the top of the page, within content sections, and at the end of blog posts or product descriptions.

The language used in CTAs should be clear and action-oriented. Use concise, persuasive text that tells users exactly what to expect when they click the CTA button.

For example: "Buy Now," "Get Started," or "Subscribe Today."

The design of CTAs should align with the website's overall style while still standing out. Experiment with different placements, button shapes, images, sizes, and colors to find what resonates best with the audience. A/B testing can provide insights into which designs and copy are most effective.

Create a sense of urgency in these CTAs when appropriate. Phrases like "Limited Time Offer" or "Only a Few Left" can motivate users to act quickly.

Ensure that the CTAs are easily clickable on mobile devices; these users should have no trouble accessing and interacting with CTAs.

Also note: A CTA that performs well on desktop might not yield the same results on a mobile device. Optimize the CTA's design for touch interactions, making sure buttons are easily clickable with a finger and that the text is still readable and looks "correct."

Each CTA is a step toward fulfilling the website's ultimate objectives. So, position and design them to create a clear, compelling pathway for user interaction.

Intuitive Navigation

Straightforward navigation is the backbone of a well-designed website. It's what guides users, helping them find the information they seek, discover products or services, and, ultimately, engage with the brand.

Users should be able to effortlessly navigate the site, finding what they need without feeling lost or overwhelmed. Intuitive navigation ensures that users can quickly access the content or products that interest them. This leads to a more satisfying and efficient experience.

- Users who can't find what they're looking for are much more likely to leave the site. Clear navigation lowers bounce rates and keeps visitors engaged.
- **Search engines also value well-organized websites**. When content is logically structured and easy to navigate, it will positively impact search engine rankings.

Crafting user-friendly navigation for a website requires a strategic approach that starts with organization. An intelligently organized website simplifies the user journey. Users can explore more content, discover products or services, and complete meaningful actions with less effort. This leads to a more satisfying and streamlined experience—a direct path to conversions.

When users find it easy to locate relevant content, they are less likely to *bounce* back to search engine results or exit the site prematurely. Lower *bounce rates* indicate that users are engaged and finding value. Google and other search engines reward websites that offer a well-structured, organized, and user-focused experience. A logical content hierarchy makes it easier for bots to crawl and index the site. It also helps search engines understand the context and relevance of its content.

Why does this matter? Because search engines are focused on delivering the most relevant and valuable content to their users.

When the site's structure clearly delineates topics and subtopics, it becomes easier for search engines to understand the subject matter and context of the pages. This understanding influences how search engines assess the site's relevance to specific user search queries.

As a result, when users search for specific topics, search engines can more confidently present your content as the relevant result.

Chapter 3:
Technical SEO

Technical SEO significantly impacts a website's visibility in search engine results.

At the heart of SEO, there is one fundamental truth: No matter how beautiful or well-crafted your strategy, the website will *only* be successful in search results if its technical foundation is solid.

Website Security (SSL/TLS)

A core aspect of technical SEO is using an SSL certificate on the website. SSL stands for Secure Sockets Layer, and an SSL certificate is a digital certificate that encrypts data exchanged between a user's web browser and a website's server. It ensures that the information transmitted between a user and a website remains private and secure.

TLS (Transport Layer Security) is the more modern version of SSL, although the term SSL is still widely used in everyday language. Even though tech has evolved, most major certificate providers still call them SSL certificates, sticking to the old-school name everyone already knows. When you get an "SSL Certificate" for the website, you're actually getting a combo deal—they're all SSL/TLS Certificates. There are no "just SSL" or "just TLS" certificates. So, if you're sweating about swapping out your SSL certificate for a TLS one, don't—it's all the same gear in the end.

When an SSL certificate is in place, it activates the HTTPS (Hypertext Transfer Protocol Secure) protocol in the website's URL (Uniform Resource Locator), typically denoted by a padlock icon in the browser's address bar. Visitors are likelier to engage with and transact on websites that display the padlock icon and use HTTPS, knowing their information is protected. As user awareness of online security grows, they increasingly expect websites to use HTTPS. This encryption makes it highly challenging for malicious actors to intercept and decipher sensitive information like login credentials, personal details, or payment information.

Search engines like Google prioritize website security. Google has confirmed that HTTPS *is* a ranking factor, meaning websites with SSL certificates have an advantage in search engine rankings.[2]

Browsers will flag non-HTTPS sites as "Not Secure," deterring users and sending them back to search results on the hunt for a secure alternative. We've all seen this in our own browser address bars at some time or another. How did it make you feel about the site? Now, imagine how someone much, much less tech-savvy, feels about being given a red warning notice that the site they were considering taking an action on is "not secure."

One significant development in recent years is the widespread availability of free SSL certificates. Many more reputable hosting providers now include complimentary SSL certificates as part of their hosting packages, making it easier than ever to secure a website.

---

[2] Google. 'HTTPS as a Ranking Signal.' Google Search Central Blog, 7 August 2014, https://developers.google.com/search/blog/2014/08/https-as-ranking-signal.

Enforce SSL/HTTPS

To safeguard data integrity, you should enforce SSL/HTTPS. It secures data transmission of internal files and prevents the mixed content warnings that scare users away. A mixed content warning occurs when a secure webpage, delivered over HTTPS, contains elements (like images, scripts, or stylesheets) served over an insecure HTTP connection.

This situation undermines the security of the entire page because the insecure elements can be exploited by attackers to intercept or alter the content, leading to potential breaches of user privacy and data security.

Here's how to proceed with enforcing SSL/HTTPS:

1. Check with Your Hosting Provider: Many hosting providers that offer SSL also provide an option to enforce SSL through your hosting control panel or dashboard, making it hassle-free.

2. Explore WordPress Plugins: If WordPress powers your website, you can explore various plugins that simplify SSL/HTTPS enforcement. Popular plugins like "Really Simple SSL" and "Let's Encrypt" streamline the process, automatically addressing mixed content issues.

Enforcing SSL/HTTPS eliminates mixed content warnings and fosters user trust. When visitors see the padlock icon or "Secure" label in their browser's address bar, they are reassured that their data is protected. This proactive approach enhances the website's security and ensures users get a smooth and secure browsing experience.

Website Crawlability

Search engines use crawlers, also known as bots or spiders, that traverse websites and index their content. When a website is crawlable, these bots can navigate it efficiently, ensuring content is indexed and ranked in search results.

Let's go over a few fundamental steps you can take to ensure these bots have full, unhindered access.

Ensure all URLs return a 200 OK status with no errors

When a URL returns a "200 OK" status, it means the server has successfully responded to the request, and the page is accessible without any server errors. This ensures that the page is technically functional and can be crawled by search engines.

To check if all URLs on the website return a "200 OK" status without errors, you can use various online tools or perform manual checks.

Google Search Console:

Google Search Console (GSC) provides a way to check for crawl errors.

1. Log in to the Search Console account.

2. Select the website property.

3. In the left-hand menu, click on "Pages" under the "Indexing" section.

Here, you'll find a list of reasons why pages aren't indexed. Look in the "Why pages aren't indexed" section.

1. Click on any specific line item error to get more details and pinpoint problematic URLs.

2. Address the issues accordingly.

Online Tools:

There are various online tools available that can check the HTTP status of multiple URLs at once.

Examples include httpstatus.io, http.app, and various other online HTTP status checkers.

1. Enter the website's URLs or sitemap URL into one of these tools.

2. The tool will crawl the URLs and provide a report showing their HTTP status codes.

3. Look for URLs that return anything other than "200 OK" and investigate the issues.

Website Auditor Tools:

Some SEO audit tools like Screaming Frog SEO Spider or Sitebulb can be installed on your computer and used to crawl a website and check for various issues, including HTTP response codes. These tools provide detailed reports of URLs with non-200 status codes.

Manual Inspection:

You can manually inspect a website by visiting each page to check for errors. Open a web browser and go through the website, clicking links and checking the address bar for any issues. As you encounter each page, ensure that it loads correctly and that the address in the browser remains consistent (e.g., no redirection to an error page or display of an error code).

Ensure only the correct URLs are fully indexable

While ensuring that all URLs return a "200 OK" status ensures technical accessibility, ensuring that all URLs are fully indexable involves thoughtful consideration of whether each page's content *should* be part of the search engine index.

Search engines rely on indexing to organize and retrieve information from the internet. When a page is indexed, it means its content is evaluated and added to the search engine's database. This enables the search engine to include the page in search results when users look for relevant information.

Of course, not all URLs on a website are meant to be indexed. Some serve purposes that aren't aligned with search engine indexing. For pages that shouldn't be indexed, using the "noindex" tag is a valuable tool in maintaining a clean and relevant search presence.

Consider pages like:

- **"Thank You" Pages**: These pages often appear after a user completes a form submission or takes a specific action on a site. They are typically used for conversion tracking; they may contain messages of gratitude or instructions for the user. However, they don't offer valuable content for search engine users and can skew conversion tracking if they receive organic traffic.
- **Checkout Pages**: Like thank-you pages, checkout pages in e-commerce sites aren't meant for search engine users.
- **Admin/Login Pages**: Pages where administrators or users log in to access the site's backend are usually not intended for public consumption. They are functional parts of the site but shouldn't be visible in search results to maintain some semblance of privacy and increase security.

When applied to a page, the "noindex" tag signals to search engines, "This page is not for public search results."

Webmasters can place the "noindex" meta tag in the HTML code of a page's header section.

```
<meta name="robots" content="noindex">
```

This tag provides explicit instructions to search engine crawlers not to index the content. Once search engines encounter the "noindex" tag on a page, they skip indexing that page's content. This means the page won't appear in SERPs.

While search engines won't index "noindex" pages, users can still access them if they have the direct URL or are directed to it. These pages are not hidden from users; they are simply excluded from search engine results.

Using the "noindex" tag also helps optimize the crawl budget for the most important and valuable content by preventing non-essential pages from being crawled.

Warning: Handle "noindex" tags with care.

While "noindex" tags are valuable tools for controlling which pages or content search engines index, they should be used judiciously. Using "noindex" on primary pages like product listings, category pages, or informational content **will harm** your SEO efforts. Such pages provide valuable information to users and help with search rankings.

So, be cautious when applying "noindex" tags, as applying them to the wrong pages or sections can inadvertently hide important content from search engines. Always double-check the pages you intend to exclude.

"Noindex" is not "Nofollow"

The "noindex" tag doesn't affect whether search engines follow links on the page. To prevent crawling and indexing, combine "noindex" with the "nofollow" tag, especially when dealing with sensitive or low-value pages.

```
<meta name="robots" content="noindex, nofollow">
```

Robots.txt vs. "Noindex"

Consider using Robots.txt, which is more effective for preventing crawling.

```
User-agent: *
Disallow: /example-directory/
Disallow: /private/
```

In this example:

- `User-agent: *` applies the rules to all search engines and web crawlers.
- `Disallow: /example-directory/` prevents search engines from accessing any page or file in the example-directory folder.
- `Disallow: /private/` prevents search engines from accessing any page or file in the `private` folder.

Place the `robots.txt` file in the root directory of your website so search engines can find and apply these rules.

Testing

Before implementing "noindex" on a large scale, it's advisable to test it on a few pages first to observe the impact on search engine visibility and user experience. Regularly audit the website for pages with "noindex" tags to ensure they still serve their intended purpose. Remove the tag if the page's role changes or if you want it to be indexed again.

Remember that SEO is a delicate balance, and while "noindex" tags can be a valuable part of your strategy, they should be used thoughtfully and strategically. Make sure you fully understand the implications before applying them to any part of your website.

Canonical URLs

Canonical URLs help search engines understand the preferred version of a page when multiple URLs point to similar content. Defining canonical URLs correctly prevents duplicate content issues and guides search engines to the most relevant pages.

Sometimes, you might have different URLs that lead to the same or very similar content on the website. This can confuse search engines because they don't know which one to show in search results. By setting a canonical URL, you're telling search engines, "When you see these similar pages, please consider this one the main source."

Properly setting canonical URLs is about making things clear and organized for search engines and website visitors.

Here are some common examples:

1. Pagination:

Websites with paginated content, such as blog archives or product listings, can create duplicate content issues across multiple pages. Canonical URLs help consolidate the content's ranking signals into a single preferred version.

Example: A blog has multiple pages for articles in a category. The canonical URL for each paginated page is set to the first page to avoid duplicate content.

2. HTTPS and HTTP Versions:

When transitioning from HTTP to HTTPS, or if both versions are accessible, canonical URLs help specify the secure version as the preferred one.

Example: A website switches from HTTP to HTTPS, but both versions are accessible. The canonical URL is set to the HTTPS version to ensure secure pages are indexed.

3. URL Parameters:

E-commerce sites often use URL parameters for sorting, filtering, or tracking purposes. Canonical URLs help avoid indexing these parameterized URLs as separate pages.

Example: An online store allows users to sort products by price, brand, or popularity, resulting in different URL parameters. The canonical URL is set to the original category page.

4. www and Non-www Versions:

Websites can be accessible with and without the "www" prefix. Canonical URLs specify the preferred version to avoid splitting ranking signals.

Example: A website can be reached at "https://example.com" and "https://www.example.com." The canonical URL is set consistently to one version.

In those examples, setting canonical URLs helps prevent duplicate content issues and ensures that search engines prioritize the correct version of a page for indexing and ranking.

Here is an example of how to implement a canonical URL:

Suppose you have two URLs that point to the same page. This may be due to tracking parameters or different session IDs:

1. http://www.example.com/product.php?item=example

2.http://www.example.com/product.php?item=example&trackingid=12

Both URLs lead to the same content, but for search engines, they appear as different pages. To prevent this duplication issue and tell search engines which URL is the master or "canonical" version, you would add a canonical link element in the <head> section of the HTML of these pages like this:

```
<link rel="canonical" href="http://www.example.com/product.php?item=example" />
```

In this example, `http://www.example.com/product.php?item=example` is the canonical URL. This tells search engines to consider this URL the primary one and ignore the others with varying parameters.

Suboptimal or Broken Links

Suboptimal or broken internal links can confuse humans and crawlers on websites of any size. These links are the pathways that connect different parts of the website, guiding users and bots through content.

Regularly check internal and external links to ensure they are error-free and reach the intended destinations. Broken links disrupt user experience by preventing visitors from accessing the desired content. This frustrates users and erodes their trust in the website in question.

To maintain a positive, seamless user experience and preserve the website's search engine ranking, regularly check and ensure that all linked URLs are error-free.

- Periodically review the website's internal and external links.
- Click on each link to confirm that it leads to the intended destination.
- Address any broken links you encounter.

Various online tools and website plugins can automatically scan a site for broken links. Popular options include "Online Broken Link Checker" and WordPress plugins like "Broken Link Checker." Platforms like Semrush offer this as part of their site audit reporting.

Screaming Frog can also help you identify and address broken link issues within a website. We mentioned Screaming Frog earlier, and you can use the free version for many of these needs as long as the site has under 500 URLs (this is the set limit of the free version).

Here's how you can use Screaming Frog to check for broken links:

1. Download and Install Screaming Frog: You can download the software from the official website and install it on your computer.

2. Crawl The Website: Open Screaming Frog and enter the website's URL in the starting address field. Click the "Start" button to begin the crawling process.

3. Review the Results: Screaming Frog will provide a detailed report of the website's status once the crawl is complete. To specifically check for broken links, go to the "Response Codes" tab. Here, you can filter the results to display "Client Error (4xx)" and "Server Error (5xx)" codes, which indicate broken links.

4. Identify Broken Links: Review the list of URLs with error codes to identify the broken links on the site.

5. Address Broken Links: After identifying the broken links, you can take action to address them. This may involve updating the links to point to the correct URLs or removing them if necessary.

Screaming Frog also examines SEO elements like page titles, meta descriptions, and heading tags, helping identify areas for optimization. This level of detailed analysis makes it an indispensable resource for website owners and SEO professionals aiming to maintain a well-functioning, error-free website with optimal visibility.

404's & Redirects

In website management, handling 404 errors – commonly known as "Page Not Found" errors – is an aspect that combines technical SEO, user experience, and site maintenance. These errors arise when a page a user or crawler requests cannot be found on the server, indicating missing or removed content.

Broken links can be more than mere inconveniences; they can signal deeper issues in a website's navigation and structure. Users encountering 404 errors may leave the site, increasing bounce rates, while search engines facing frequent 404s may deem the site less reliable, affecting its ranking.

Websites are living entities that change, including URL modifications, content updates, and structural reorganizations. Redirects ensure that these changes occur smoothly from a user's perspective, seamlessly guiding them through the website's evolving landscape. A redirect is a method implemented on a web server or via client-side code that automatically takes users and crawlers from one URL to another.

Regularly inspecting a website's internal link structure will help locate any links leading to URLs that return 404 errors. These should be updated, redirecting users to the correct, existing pages. This is a step in maintaining the site's internal navigational integrity.

Testing redirects is a step post-implementation or post-modification. This involves manually visiting the old URLs to confirm they direct to the new destinations seamlessly, as expected. Utilizing online tools and browser extensions designed for redirect testing provides an additional layer of scrutiny, helping to detect and resolve any anomalies or inefficiencies in the redirection process.

The upkeep of redirects is a continuous obligation. As a website's content evolves, URLs change and new pages are added, so redirects must be updated accordingly. Redirects are not a one-size-fits-all solution; they require careful implementation through various methods suited to specific scenarios and technical environments.

Types of Redirects

The variety of redirects available are not just a matter of choice but a strategic decision-making process that hinges on a website's specific goals and requirements. Whether it's a permanent shift in content location, a temporary change due to site maintenance, or a more complex scenario requiring *method and body consistency in requests*, each redirect type serves a unique purpose. These distinctions are not merely technical but deeply intertwined with how search engines interpret and respond to these redirects, directly impacting a website's search performance.

301 Redirect - Permanent Redirect

A 301 redirect is an HTTP status code that informs web browsers and search engines that a web page has moved permanently to a new location. It is implemented on the server side and can be set up in various ways, depending on the server type (e.g., editing the .htaccess file on Apache servers). The 301 status code is an essential part of HTTP protocol and is recognized by all major web browsers and search engines.

From an SEO perspective, a 301 redirect is critical because it transfers the majority of the original page's link equity (ranking power) to the new URL. This feature is ideal for changing domain names, migrating to HTTPS, or restructuring a website where the old URL will no longer be used. It is also used when consolidating multiple pages into one (for example, after merging two similar articles into a comprehensive guide).

302 Redirect - Found/Temporary Redirect

The 302 redirect is an HTTP status code indicating a temporary redirection of a webpage. Unlike the 301 redirect, the 302 tells search engines that the original URL should be retained in their index, as the move is only temporary. It is also a server-side redirect and can be implemented in similar ways to a 301 redirect.

A 302 redirect does not pass significant link equity from the original page to the new one. It's typically used when a page's content is temporarily moved, but there's an intention to return it to the original URL. Overusing or incorrectly using 302 redirects can cause SEO issues, such as diluted page ranking or content indexing problems.

These are commonly used during website maintenance or when a page is undergoing significant updates and has been temporarily moved to another location. It is also useful for A/B testing scenarios where users are shown different page versions for a short period.

307 Redirect - Temporary Redirect (HTTP 1.1)

A 307 redirect is an HTTP 1.1 successor of the 302 redirect and is used to indicate a temporary redirect like its predecessor. The key difference is that a 307 redirect guarantees that the method and the body of the original request are not changed when the request is redirected.

"Method" and "Body" refer to components of HTTP requests made when accessing web pages:

1. Method: This refers to the HTTP method used in the request. The most common HTTP methods are GET, POST, PUT, DELETE, etc. Each method indicates a different action or request being made to the server. For example, GET is used to request data from a specified resource, and POST is used to submit data to be processed to a specified resource, and so on.

2. Body: This refers to the data part of an HTTP request or response. In the case of requests, the body typically contains data you want to send to the server. This is particularly relevant for methods like POST or PUT, which often include data payloads (the body) that contain information the server needs to process, such as form data or file uploads.

"Method and body consistency in requests" means ensuring that during the redirection process (whether permanent or temporary), the type of request (GET, POST, etc.) and the data sent in the request (the body) are consistently maintained. This is important because different types of redirects change how these elements are treated or forwarded to the new location, which could lead to errors or unintended behavior if not handled correctly.

Like 302 redirects, 307 redirects do not pass significant link equity to the new URL. They are less common than 301 and 302 redirects and are primarily seen in more complex web applications where it's important to keep the data sending and receiving methods consistent.

Meta Refresh

Meta Refresh is a redirect executed on the client side using a meta tag in the HTML head section. It allows a web page to be automatically refreshed or redirected after a specified number of seconds. While technically not an HTTP status code redirect, it is used for similar purposes.

Meta Refresh redirects are generally **not recommended** for SEO purposes. Since they rely on the browser to execute the redirect, they are slower and less efficient than server-side redirects like 301 or 302. This can confuse users as well as search engines. They also do not pass link equity effectively and can lead to issues with search indexing, as search engines may not always interpret them like server-side redirects.

Redirect Issues & Management

The management of redirects involves continuous monitoring, testing, and optimizing to ensure that they serve their intended purpose effectively. If not correctly managed, redirects can lead to complex issues that negatively impact user experience and search engine rankings.

Looping Redirects

These occur when a redirect inadvertently points back to itself or creates a cycle with another redirect, resulting in an endless loop. Such loops are not just confusing for users, leading to frustrating experiences, but they also present significant obstacles for crawlers, hindering efficient indexing of content.

To prevent this, regular audits of redirect chains are necessary. These involve mapping out the path of each redirect to ensure that it leads to the correct destination without any loops or unnecessary detours.

Broken Redirects

A broken redirect occurs when a URL redirects to a non-existent or incorrect page, leading users (and bots) to a dead end. This issue can arise from site restructuring, deleted pages, or typographical errors in redirect rules. Frequent assessments through webmaster tools and crawl analysis tools are indispensable in identifying and rectifying such broken redirects.

Redirect Chains

The complexity of redirect management is further heightened when dealing with multiple redirects, known as redirect chains. While redirect chains are sometimes necessary for things like temporary site migrations, dealing with legacy systems, affiliate marketing, or to satisfy specific policy or legal requirements, their efficiency is critical:

- Each step in a redirect chain should be purposeful, using 301 or 302 redirects as appropriate based on whether the move is permanent or temporary.

- The chain should be as short as possible, leading users and bots to the final destination with minimal delay.

Optimizing redirect chains enhances user experience and conserves the crawl budget allotted by search engines, ensuring that the site's most important content is crawled and indexed effectively.

Tools For Assessing Redirect Health

1. Screaming Frog SEO Spider - A comprehensive tool that crawls websites to identify redirect chains and loops, 404 errors, and other common issues. It's excellent for both small (free version covers most small sites) and large (with the paid version) websites.

2. Redirect Path (Chrome Extension) - A browser extension that flags 301, 302, 404, and 500 HTTP Status Codes and other issues like meta-refresh redirects. It's useful for quick checks while browsing.

3. Semrush Site Audit - Offers a thorough website audit, including redirect issues, allowing you to identify and fix problems that could impact your SEO performance.

4. Ahrefs Site Audit - Provides a detailed site audit feature that can identify redirect issues, such as broken redirects, redirect loops, and temporary redirects that should be permanent.

5. Moz Pro Site Crawl - This tool crawls your site to identify various issues, including broken redirects and chains of redirects, helping you maintain a healthy website structure.

6. Google Search Console - Offers insights into how Google views your website, including crawl errors that can arise from problematic redirects. It's essential for understanding your site's performance in Google search.

7. HTTP Status Code Checker Tool - Various online tools can check the status codes of URLs in bulk, which is helpful for quickly identifying redirect issues across your site.

8. Lumar (Formerly DeepCrawl) - A cloud-based crawler that comprehensively analyzes your website, identifying redirect issues, broken links, and opportunities for optimization.

Each tool offers unique features to help webmasters and SEO professionals monitor and manage redirects effectively.

Page Load Optimization

Page load speed is the time it takes for a web page to render fully in a user's browser. It measures how fast all the text, images, scripts, and interactive elements come together to present a coherent and visually appealing web page.

And make no mistake, this time matters immensely. Slow-loading pages frustrate users, increasing bounce rates and signaling to search engines that the website may not provide a satisfactory experience.

Users have grown accustomed to instant gratification. They expect web pages to load seamlessly and without any delays. When a user clicks on the website but is met with a sluggish loading process, seconds feel like minutes. Frustration sets in, and the likelihood of them leaving the site increases with each passing moment.

This phenomenon is captured by a metric known as the bounce rate. A high bounce rate indicates that visitors are landing on a page and promptly navigating away without engaging further. Slow page loading times are a significant contributor to elevated bounce rates. When users encounter delays, they often conclude that the website is unreliable or unable to meet their needs, prompting them to seek alternatives.

However, the repercussions of slow-loading pages extend beyond elevated bounce rates. Slow-loading pages can foster a negative brand perception that lingers long after the user has departed. When users encounter a frustrating online experience, they are more likely to associate that frustration with the brand itself.

In turn, all of this will negatively impact search rankings. This phenomenon is rooted in the logic of user satisfaction. Search engines aim to present users with the most relevant, reliable, and engaging content in response to their queries. When a user initiates a search query, search engines race against the clock to present relevant results promptly. Fast-loading pages meet the user's expectation of efficiency, thus aligning with search engines' goal of providing swift access to information.

Crawl Budget and Page Speed

Search engine crawlers have a limited amount of time and resources allocated to their task. This allocation is what we refer to as *crawl budget*.

Page load speed can augment or deplete this finite SEO resource:

- - Fast-loading pages allow search engine crawlers to use their budget efficiently, covering more of the site in less time.
- - Slow-loading pages consume more of this budget, limiting the crawler's ability to explore other areas of the site.

This issue is not just theoretical; it has real consequences for a website's visibility. When crawlers dedicate an excessive portion of their budget to slow-loading pages, they leave less room for other essential tasks, such as indexing new content, analyzing updates, or revisiting previously indexed pages.

Factors Influencing Page Speed

1. Large Images and Media:

- High-resolution images and videos can drastically impede page loading times. Reducing the file size of media assets without sacrificing quality is imperative.

- Image optimization techniques include compression, resizing, and using modern file formats like WebP.

2. Unoptimized Code:

- Complex or unoptimized code, such as JavaScript and CSS, can hinder page speed. Minification and combining of these files can reduce their size and HTTP requests.

- Efficient coding practices, like asynchronous loading of scripts, can further enhance page performance.

3. Server Performance:

- The quality of the web hosting server significantly influences page load times. Opting for a reputable hosting provider and upgrading to a faster server when necessary can yield performance improvements.

4. External Resources:

- Relying on external resources, like scripts or stylesheets hosted on third-party domains, can introduce delays if these resources load slowly.

- Consider hosting critical resources locally or on a Content Delivery Network (CDN) for faster access.

5. Browser Caching:

- Proper browser caching settings allow repeat visitors to load a site more swiftly by storing static resources locally.

- Implementing HTTP caching headers and setting cache expiration times are intelligent strategies.

Optimizing page speed is a key component of your SEO strategy, as it boosts user experience and ensures seamless crawling by search engines, contributing significantly to the website's overall performance.

Structured Data & Metadata

The Internet uses structured data and metadata to organize and interpret vast amounts of web content. Structured data refers to any data that is organized and formatted predictably, making it easily understood and processed by search engines. Metadata, on the other hand, provides information about the data on a webpage, describing its content, creator, purpose, and more. Together, structured data and metadata guide search engines, helping them to crawl, understand, and display content effectively.

Schema Markup

Schema markup is code you put in a page to help search engines return more detailed or informative results. It tells search engines what the data means, not just what it says. Schema was developed through a collaborative effort between Google, Bing, Yahoo, and Yandex, represented by Schema.org. The mission was to create a standard set of *schemas* for structured data markup on pages across the internet.

While the content on a website gets indexed and returned in search results, as most of us are used to, with Schema markup, some content gets indexed and served in a different way. These schemas, or vocabularies, help search engines understand the context of the content on a page, enabling them to provide richer, more informative results for users.

For instance, if you've ever seen rich snippets in search results, you've witnessed Schema markup in action. When you see the star ratings for a product, the image of the author, the preparation time, etc., directly in the search results, that's Schema markup.

Schema.org provides a plethora of markup types, catering to various content categories. Some common types of Schema tags include:

1. Organization: This markup provides information about an organization, like a company or NGO. It can include the organization's official name, logo, contact information, and social profile links.

2. Person: This is used to detail information about an individual. It can include a person's name, job title, works for, and contact information.

3. LocalBusiness: For local businesses, this markup helps provide specific information like address, phone number, operating hours, and ratings. It's beneficial for local SEO.

4. Product & Offer: These provide details like price, availability, and reviews.

5. Article: For news and blog posts, this markup includes the article's headline, body, author, and publish date.

6. Event: For event listings, this includes details like date, location, and ticket information.

7. Recipe: This includes ingredients, cooking time, nutritional information, and ratings.

Each type enhances specific content pieces, making them more visible and attractive in search engine results.

Here are some examples of schema markup:

Local Business Schema:

```
{"@context": "http://schema.org",
```

```
  "@type": "LocalBusiness",
  "name": "Your Business Name",
  "address": {
    "@type": "PostalAddress",
    "streetAddress": "1234 Street Name",
    "addressLocality": "City",
    "addressRegion": "State",
    "postalCode": "12345"
  },
  "telephone": "+1234567890",
  "openingHours": "Mo-Fr 09:00-17:00",
  "url": "http://examplewebsite.com"}
```

Article Schema:

```
{"@context": "http://schema.org",
  "@type": "Article",
  "headline": "Title of The Article",
  "author": {
    "@type": "Person",
    "name": "Author Name"
  },
  "datePublished": "2020-01-01",
  "image": "http://www.example.com/image.jpg",
  "articleBody": "This is a short version of the
article content."}
```

There are many types of schema markups available depending on the content of the website, such as recipes, reviews, products, and more. Make sure to select the one that best suits your needs.

Dublin Core Metadata

Dublin Core is a set of vocabulary terms used to describe a wide range of web-based *resources*. Developed by the Dublin Core Metadata Initiative (DCMI), these standards are designed to facilitate the finding, sharing, and management of information across domains.[3] Dublin Core has found significant relevance in educational and government websites due to its ability to standardize information in an easily accessible manner.

The core idea behind Dublin Core (no pun intended) is its simplicity and universality, making it easily understand-able and implementable across different types of institut-ions and platforms. While Google continues to recognize Dublin Core due to its significant validations when in use for these types of information platforms, Schema Markup remains the preferred metadata schema for search market-ing purposes on most websites. This is because Schema Markup provides a more extensive framework for marking up different types of content and entities on the web. The structured data allows search engines to crawl, understand, and index the content more effectively, improving the relevance of search results.

For instance, with Schema Markup, websites achieve rich snippets in SERPs. These rich snippets can include additional information such as ratings, prices, availability, and more, which are not possible with Dublin Core. From an SEO perspective, Schema Markup aims to make it easier for search engines to 'understand' what a website and its pages are about.[4] This clearer understanding can lead to better indexing and, as a result, better rankings. While Dublin Core is also used for metadata, its scope and specificity for SEO purposes are not as developed as Schema Markup.

---

[3] Dublin Core Metadata Initiative. 'Dublin Core™ Metadata Element Set, Version 1.1: Reference Description.' 14 June 2012, https://www.dublincore.org/ specifications/dublin-core/dces/.
[4] "About Schema.org." Schema.org FAQ, Schema.org, n.d., https://schema.org/ docs/faq.html.

The Dublin Core standard encompasses metadata elements that offer a broad and generic range of descriptors. These elements can be used to describe physical resources like books or CDs and digital materials such as websites, documents, and multimedia.

Dublin Core fills a critical role in educational institutions, where efficient organization and retrieval of scholarly and instructional materials are the priority. It helps libraries, digital repositories, and archives to describe and index their collections accurately. For government websites, Dublin Core metadata ensures that public documents, policies, reports, and data are organized in a manner that is both accessible and understandable to the public and other government entities.

This standardization helps maintain transparency and facilitates information retrieval in the public sector. The Dublin Core schema comprises 15 basic elements, but here we'll focus on a few key ones to illustrate their application:

1. **Title**: The name of the resource.

Example: `<meta name="DC.title" content="City Environmental Policies 2021" />`

2. **Creator**: The entity primarily responsible for creating the content.

Example: `<meta name="DC.creator" content="Department of Environmental Protection" />`

3. **Subject**: The topic of the resource.

Example: `<meta name="DC.subject" content="Environmental Protection, Sustainability Policies" />`

4. **Description**: A description of the content of the resource.

Example: `<meta name="DC.description" content="Detailed report on the sustainability policies implemented in the city for the year 2021." />`

5. Publisher: The entity responsible for making the resource available.

Example: `<meta name="DC.publisher" content="City Council Publications" />`

6. Date: A date associated with the creation or availability of the resource.

Example: `<meta name="DC.date" content="2021-04-15" />`

7. Format: The file format or physical medium of the resource.

Example: `<meta name="DC.format" content="PDF" />`

To implement Dublin Core metadata, you would typically add these `<meta>` tags to the `<head>` section of HTML documents. These tags are quickly processed by browsers, search engines, and other web services, enhancing the discoverability and organization of content. By adopting these standards, *educational* and *government* institutions can significantly enhance the accessibility and management of digital content.

OpenGraph Tags

OpenGraph is an internet protocol introduced by Facebook in 2010, which allows a page to become a rich object in a social graph. Essentially, it's a standard for web pages that allows them to become a richer part of the social media ecosystem. When a link is shared on platforms like Facebook, LinkedIn, Slack, and Pinterest, OpenGraph tags determine how the page's information is displayed — the title, image, description, and more.

By integrating OpenGraph tags into a website's HTML, you can control what information shows up when someone shares the content on social media. This enhances the look of the shared content and can significantly improve CTRs and overall engagement.

Breakdown of OpenGraph Tags

1. og:title: This tag specifies the content's title as you want it to appear within the social graph. It's similar to a meta title tag but specifically for social media.

Example: `<meta property="og:title" content="10 Innovative Gardening Tips to Transform Your Home Garden" />`

2. og:type: This tag indicates the type of content being shared. Defining the content type helps social platforms present the content appropriately, whether it's an article, video, or image.

Example: `<meta property="og:type" content="article" />` for a blog post or news article.

3. og:image: One of the most influential tags, it determines the image displayed when content is shared. This should be a compelling image that represents the linked content.

Example: `<meta property="og:image" content="http://example.com/image.jpg" />`

4. og:url: This tag defines the canonical URL of the content. It helps to ensure content integrity when shared on social media.

Example: `<meta property="og:url" content="http://example.com/page.html" />`

5. og:description: Similar to a meta description, this tag briefly describes the content in the link.

Example: `<meta property="og:description" content="Explore our top 10 innovative gardening tips to bring a new lease of life to your home garden." />`

6. og:site_name: This tag is used to identify the name of the website or application.

Example: `<meta property="og:site_name" content="GreenThumb Gardening" />`

Best Practices

1. Use High-Quality Images: For the `og:image` tag, use high-resolution images that are visually appealing as they play a primary role in user engagement.

2. Optimize Content for Different Platforms: Different social media platforms have varying specifications for how they display OpenGraph content. It's wise to tailor OpenGraph tags to suit the primary platforms the target audience uses.

3. Consistency in Information: Ensure that the information provided in OpenGraph tags is consistent with the content on the page. Misleading tags can result in lower engagement and trust.

4. Testing and Validation: Use tools like Facebook's Sharing Debugger to preview how content will appear on Facebook and debug any issues with the OpenGraph tags.

5. Regular Updates: Keep OpenGraph tags updated, especially the images and descriptions, to stay aligned with page content changes or updates.

Through careful tag crafting, you can ensure that the content looks appealing when shared, encourages interaction, and drives traffic back to the site.

Twitter Cards

Even though it's the X platform now, Twitter Cards allow you to attach rich media to tweets beyond the confines of the character limit. When a tweet contains a link to a webpage where the Twitter Card code is implemented, the tweet can display additional information directly within the Twitter feed, such as a preview image, a title, and a description.

This feature is particularly important for enhancing user engagement on X (Twitter), as it makes the content more appealing and informative, encouraging higher CTRs and interactions. Using Twitter Cards, content creators can ensure their shared content stands out in a busy X feed. They provide a more immersive experience, allowing users to get a glimpse of what the link contains before clicking.

There are several types of Twitter Cards, each designed to for different types of content:

1. Summary Card: This is the most basic type of Twitter Card and includes a title, description, thumbnail, and Twitter account attribution. It's suitable for blog posts, news articles, and product pages.

Example: `<meta name="twitter:card" content="summary" />`

2. Summary Card with Large Image: Similar to the Summary Card but with a larger, more prominent image. This card is particularly effective for visually driven content.

Example: `<meta name="twitter:card" content="summary_large_image" />`

3. App Card: Designed for mobile app promotion, it allows for direct download of an app from the tweet.

Example: `<meta name="twitter:card" content="app" />`

4. Player Card: Used for media-rich content like videos and audio clips, allowing them to be played directly within the tweet.

Example: `<meta name="twitter:card" content="player" />`

Implementing Twitter Cards involves adding specific HTML meta tags to a web page's <head> section. For example:

```
<meta name="twitter:card"
content="summary_large_image">

<meta name="twitter:site"
content="@twitterhandle">
```

```
<meta name="twitter:title" content="Title of
The Content">
```

```
<meta name="twitter:description" content="Brief
description of the content">
```

```
<meta name="twitter:image" content="URL of a
relevant image">
```

To note, many CMS platforms offer plugins that handle this, including RankMath for WordPress.

Validate The Card: Use X's Twitter Card Validator tool to test and preview the Twitter Card.

Regularly Update The Cards: Keep Twitter Cards updated in line with any changes to the content, especially the images and descriptions.

XML Sitemaps

An XML sitemap is a structured file that lists a website's URLs. This file follows the Extensible Markup Language (XML) format, a markup language much like HTML but designed to store and transport data. In simple terms, it is a roadmap of a website that guides search engines through the site's content, ensuring they are aware of all available pages.

The structure of an XML sitemap is fairly simple but must adhere to a protocol set by search engines like Google. The basic elements of an XML sitemap include:

- `<urlset>`: The parent tag enclosing the entire list of URLs.
- `<url>`: Each URL listed in the sitemap is contained within this tag.
- `<loc>`: Within each <url> tag, this specifies the webpage's location (URL).
- `<lastmod>`: This optional tag provides the page's last modification date.

- `<changefreq>`: Also optional, indicating how frequently the page content will likely change.
- `<priority>`: An optional attribute suggesting the page's importance relative to other URLs in the sitemap.

Impact on Search Rankings

While simply having an XML sitemap itself is not a direct ranking factor, its indirect influence on search rankings is substantial:

1. Improved Indexing: By aiding in indexing all relevant pages, a sitemap can expedite a site's visibility in SERPs.

2. Page Prioritization: Through the `<priority>` tag, you can suggest which pages should be considered more important, potentially influencing how search engines prioritize content during indexing.

3. Content Freshness: Regularly updated sitemaps signal to search engines that the site is active and regularly refreshed, which can be a positive signal for ranking.

4. Enhanced Crawl Efficiency: Efficient crawling due to a well-structured sitemap means that search engines can quickly find and index valuable content.

Sitemap Creation and Optimization Steps

1. Creating an XML Sitemap:

Start by generating an XML sitemap for the website. You can use various tools and plugins to automate this process, depending on your content management system (CMS).

In WordPress, plugins like Yoast SEO and Rank Math can generate sitemaps for you. Automatic integrations or online sitemap generators are available for other platforms or custom-built websites.

Here is what an XML sitemap file format looks like:

```
<?xml version="1.0" encoding="UTF-8"?>
<urlset
xmlns="http://www.sitemaps.org/schemas/sitemap/
0.9">
    <url>
        <loc>https://www.example.com/</loc>
        <lastmod>2024-02-25</lastmod>
        <changefreq>daily</changefreq>
        <priority>1.0</priority>
    </url>
    <!-- Add more URLs as necessary -->
</urlset>
```

2. Review the Sitemap Structure:

Once you have the sitemap, review its structure carefully. Verifying that it includes all the pages you want search engines to index. This typically includes main content pages, blog posts, product pages, images, and other relevant content.

3. Prioritize Important Pages:

Within the sitemap, prioritize important pages by placing them higher in the hierarchy. This helps crawlers understand which pages are more critical and should be crawled more frequently. This may not be possible with some automated tools.

4. Ensure Clean URLs:

Check that all URLs listed in the sitemap are clean, concise, and representative of the content they lead to. Avoid including URLs with parameters or confusing characters.

5. Eliminate Redirect Chains:

If there are any redirect chains within the sitemap, resolve them. Redirect chains slow down the crawling process and can lead to errors.

6. Ensure Consistent URLs:

Ensure consistency between the URLs in the sitemap and the actual URLs of the web pages. Any discrepancies can confuse search engines.

7. Validate XML Sitemap:

Use online XML sitemap validators or tools provided by search engines (e.g., Google's Search Console) to validate the XML sitemap. This will help identify any structural or syntax errors.

8. Keep It Updated:

As you add or remove pages from the website, update the XML sitemap accordingly. An outdated sitemap can mislead search engines. Most automated solutions cover this for you.

9. Create an HTML Sitemap:

Consider creating an HTML sitemap as well, especially if it is a large website. This can aid both search engines and human visitors in navigating the site.

10. Multi-Page Sitemaps:

If the website has a significant number of pages, you may need to create a sitemap index that organizes multiple sitemaps. This is useful for e-commerce websites or large publication sites.

11. Submit to Search Engines

Having crafted a website's XML sitemap by neatly organizing the site's structure, making it a cinch for search engines to understand and index the content of the site, it's time to connect it to the big players in the search game: Google Search Console, Bing Webmaster Tools, and Yandex Webmaster.

These three are like the gatekeepers of internet traffic, each with its realm of influence. By connecting the sitemap to these services, you're tapping into their vast networks, increasing visibility across a broader audience. You'll also gain valuable insights into how the site performs on these platforms. Making it easier to understand potential issues that could affect visibility.

Chapter 4:
On-Page SEO

On-page SEO refers to optimizing individual web pages to rank higher in search engines and earn more relevant traffic.

On-page SEO is about making a site more understandable and accessible for search engines and users. When executed correctly, on-page SEO ensures that search engines can easily interpret the subject and depth of web pages while providing users with a pleasant and informative experience.

Search engines want to provide the most relevant, high-quality content to users. To do this, they rely on complex algorithms that analyze a multitude of on-page factors. By optimizing these elements, you signal to search engines that the content is relevant, authoritative, and deserving of high visibility in search.

At the heart of on-page SEO lies a mission-critical understanding: understanding how search engines work. Search engines perform three primary functions: crawling, indexing, and ranking.

1. Crawling: This is the discovery stage. Search engines deploy bots (also known as crawlers) to discover new and updated content. These crawlers move through the web by following links from one page to another, gathering data about those pages.

2. Indexing: After a page is crawled, it's stored in a massive database called an index. This process involves analyzing the page's content and categorizing it based on keywords, content type, and other factors.

3. Ranking: When a user searches, the search engine sifts through its index to provide the most relevant results. This ranking is based on various factors, including keyword relevance, content quality, user experience, etc.

In the early days of SEO, search engines relied heavily on keyword matching and density to rank pages. This led to crude tactics like *keyword stuffing*, where websites would overload their content with keywords to manipulate rankings. Such tactics, you might remember, turned many web pages into jumbles of repetitive and often nonsensical keyword lists rather than resources with valuable information.

For example, a page about 'fishing tips' might awkwardly repeat 'fishing tips' multiple times in every sentence, disregarding readability or context, transforming what could otherwise be informative content into an unreadable, keyword-laden mess.

Some "SEOs" still attempt keyword stuffing to this day. However, this approach persists mainly due to a lack of understanding of current SEO best practices or a deliberate choice to use reckless SEO tactics as a result of pure laziness. In any case, as algorithms advanced, such tactics became obsolete, ineffective, and ultimately detrimental.

Significant updates over the years have shifted the focus to more nuanced factors:

- **Google Panda (2011):** Targeted low-quality content, reducing the rank of 'thin,' low-value content sites.
- **Google Penguin (2012):** Focused on penalizing sites that used manipulative link practices.
- **Google Hummingbird (2013):** Enhanced the understanding of natural language, context, and user intent.

- **RankBrain (2015):** Introduced machine learning to interpret search queries and deliver more relevant results.

These advancements have significantly impacted on-page SEO strategies. The focus has shifted from mere keyword optimization to creating high-quality, relevant, and user-first content. Modern SEO is no longer about gaming the system but aligning with search engines' sophisticated, user-focused criteria.

Keyword Research

Good keyword research involves more than just identifying basic words and phrases to incorporate into website content. It requires understanding the target audience's language when searching for the products, services, or information a site offers.

By identifying and understanding this language, you can tailor a website's content to align with specific user queries, thereby improving visibility in search engine results for the right crowd.

- **Aligning with User Search Intent**: Effective keyword research reveals the search intent behind queries. This insight allows you to create content that answers users' questions, solves their problems, or fulfills their needs.
- **Competitive Analysis**: Understanding the keywords for which your competitors rank can provide insights into market trends and content gaps you can fill.
- **Content Strategy Development**: Keyword research guides the creation of focused, relevant content that speaks directly to your audience's interests and needs.

Crafting the perfect keyword strategy for a website involves a meticulous refinement process beyond merely compiling an extensive list. At the core of this refinement is ensuring that every keyword you select is tightly aligned with the site's goals and resonates with the audience's interests.

But it doesn't stop there.

The effectiveness of your chosen keywords also hinges on their search volume—a delicate balance of aiming for keywords popular enough to guarantee visibility yet not so saturated with competition that ranking becomes a Herculean task. Search volume is a data point that many keyword research and tracking tools will provide for you. It's an overall average of traffic that the particular keyword drives on a monthly basis.

However, as with everything, keywords and interest can have seasonal highs and lows. A keyword with an average monthly search volume of 640, for instance, may actually mean low or no traffic for that keyword for several months, then several months of thousands of searches - matching seasonal interest in the topic. That "640" is just the year-end average of overall traffic divided by 12. Keyword research tools are indispensable to help you deal with this. These tools can help you gauge the search volume, seasonality, and ranking difficulty.

Tools like SEMrush or Ahrefs are particularly great at offering a glimpse into the battlefield of keyword rankings. They provide insights into how challenging it might be to secure a top spot in search results for each term by rating it on a scale of 1 (very easy) to 100 (incredibly difficult).

Many "niche" and "long tail" search terms have low search volume, and these tools will often return no data in that column if the total volume of searches is too low. (We'll discuss long tail keywords a couple of pages from now.)

These 3rd party tools also each weigh "ranking difficulty" differently, and exactly how they arrive at their numbers can range from "vague" to "proprietary secret." Thus, combining the data from more than one tool can be a better guide for evaluating how hard a keyword may be to rank for.

SEMrush, Ahrefs, SpyFu, and Moz

These platforms go beyond mere keyword suggestions; they delve into the intricacies of each keyword, offering variations, synonyms, and related phrases that significantly expand the depth of your research efforts.

The significant advantage of these tools is their ability to conduct thorough competitor analysis. They enable you to peek into competitors' keyword strategies, giving you a clear picture of the keywords they are ranking for. This competitive intelligence can help shape your SEO strategy, as it lets you uncover opportunities to outperform the competition.

Google Keyword Planner

The Google Keyword Planner is a traditional search marketer tool for generating keyword ideas and understanding their potential impact. This tool is only accessible through an active Google Ads account (with Expert Mode turned on). This information can serve as a useful proxy for organic search competition, helping you gauge how hard it might be to rank for specific keywords organically.

When you input a word or phrase into the *Keyword Ideas* tab, it doesn't just list similar keywords; it opens a window into the different ways users search around the topic. This feature is valuable for broadening your keyword list, ensuring you cover various angles and user queries related to the niche.

It also offers an estimated monthly search volume for each keyword and will project this traffic for each month individually - following seasonal demand based on historical performance in the *Forecast* tab. This data aids in gauging the popularity and potential traffic each keyword could bring to the website at any time.

Answer The Public

Answer The Public offers a unique approach to keyword research by focusing on question-based keywords. When you input a broad keyword into this tool, it generates a visual map of questions and phrases that users are asking about that topic. The tool's ability to uncover long-tail, conversational queries is particularly beneficial.

*These questions can be great for creating FAQ sections as well.

Google Trends

Google Trends is a tool for understanding the temporal dynamics of keywords. It provides a visual representation of the activity surrounding a search term over time, offering valuable insights into trending topics and seasonal fluctuations in search interest.

You can use Google Trends to identify when specific keywords are more popular and plan content accordingly. It's also helpful in spotting emerging trends in a niche, allowing you to stay ahead of the curve by creating content around these burgeoning topics. This tool can be instrumental in keeping your content strategy aligned with the target audience's evolving interests and search behaviors.

By combining the insights from each of these tools, you can develop a well-rounded and effective keyword strategy that drives traffic and deeply resonates with the target audience.

Creating an Effective Keyword List

This list forms the backbone of your on-page SEO strategy, guiding content creation and overall website optimization. Start with a brainstorming session. Leverage your familiarity with the niche or the insights you've gained through research. List potential topics, questions, and pain points the audience might have.

Divide your brainstormed topics into categories based on the identified user intents:

- **Informational Intent**: These are topics where users seek knowledge. Example keywords might be "how to live eco-friendly," "benefits of sustainable living," or "best energy-saving practices."

- **Transactional Intent**: These keywords are used when users are ready to purchase. Examples might include "buy eco-friendly kitchenware," "sustainable clothing stores," or "affordable solar panels."

- **Navigational Intent**: This category is brand-specific, such as "GreenLife blog" or "EcoWorld product reviews."

Incorporate Long-Tail Keywords, which are longer, more specific phrases that precisely capture the user's intent. They tend to have lower search volumes but higher conversion rates due to their specificity.

Example:

Regular Keyword: used cars for sale

Long-Tail Keyword: used family cars for sale under $5000 in Miami

Organizing and Prioritizing

Organize your list by grouping similar keywords and prioritizing them based on your initial ideas for a content strategy. Start with highly relevant keywords with a balanced ratio of search volume to competition.

Creating a keyword list is a strategic process that intertwines your understanding of the niche and user intent. This list will be the foundation upon which you build your content, tailor the website, and, ultimately, reach the audience more effectively. With that in mind, keep your keyword list fluid. Don't set just a static list of 10-20 high-priority targets and call it a campaign; track all targets chosen initially and along the campaign's life as they are discovered.

Low-volume keywords that are very niche-specific can act as overall health indicators. While the desired large targets may seem like they are not moving very well initially, these relevant and neighboring low-volume keywords can show an overall and nuanced progression toward those larger goals.

Page and Content Optimization

Now that we have identified our target keywords, the next step in on-page SEO is optimizing the content on the website's main pages. Content is the primary medium through which keywords are conveyed, significantly influencing how search engines and users perceive a website. This stage is not just about embedding keywords; the aim is to produce SEO-friendly content that enhances site visibility and user engagement.

Developing an SEO-friendly content structure requires a blend of understanding the audience, satisfying user intent, and maintaining quality and readability. Content should be well-written, jargon-free, and broken down into easily digestible segments. This approach aids in user retention and facilitates easier content consumption.

Effective content structuring is about organizing content so that it's easy for users to read and for search engines to understand.

- **Logical Flow**: Arrange content in a logical order. Start with an introduction that sets the stage for the content, then a body that delves into the details, and conclude with a summary or call-to-action.

- **Paragraphs and Sentences**: Keep paragraphs and sentences short and to the point. Long, unwieldy paragraphs can deter readers and make the content less digestible.
- **Bullet Points and Lists**: Use bullet points or numbered lists where appropriate. They can make complex information more accessible and highlight key points or steps effectively.
- **Visual Elements**: Use images, videos, and graphics to break up text and add visual interest. These elements can enhance user engagement and provide alternative ways to present information.
- **Whitespace**: Don't underestimate the power of whitespace. Ample spacing between paragraphs and around elements can significantly improve a page's readability and overall aesthetic.

Headings

Structuring content with clear headings and subheadings ensures readability and helps search engines understand the content's hierarchy and importance. Heading tags, ranging from H1 to H6, serve as a hierarchical representation of the content's structure. They help search engines understand the organization and priority of the information on the page.

The H1 tag, typically the page's title, is the most important. It's the first indicator to a search engine and users of the page's primary focus. Subsequent headers, H2, H3, and so on, act as subheadings that further break down the content into digestible sections, each addressing different but related subtopics.

From an SEO perspective, header tags provide context and structure, making it easier for search engines to crawl and index pages effectively. They also play a role in keyword optimization, as headers are the primary places to integrate relevant keywords and phrases.

Use of Header Tags for SEO

1. Prioritizing H1 Tags: Each main page or landing page should have one, and only one, H1 tag. This tag should clearly and concisely describe the overall topic of the page. It's usually the same or a variation of the page title and should contain your primary target keyword.

2. Utilizing H2 and H3 Tags for Structure: Use H2 tags for the main subsections of the content. These tags are perfect for including secondary keywords and providing structure to a page. H3 tags can be used for sub-sections within these H2 sections, adding another level of hierarchy and detail.

3. Keyword Integration: Incorporate relevant keywords into the header tags, but do so naturally. Avoid keyword stuffing, and ensure that the inclusion of keywords does not compromise the readability or relevance of the headers.

4. Reflecting the Content's Flow: Your header tags should reflect the natural flow and progression of the content. They should guide the reader through the page, creating a logical and intuitive structure that enhances user experience.

Keyword research and optimization in the context of on-page SEO are about much more than mere keyword insertion; it's about crafting content that resonates with and fulfills the needs of your audience. If you use an SEO tool with the keyword density function turned on, shut it off. The frequency of keyword usage is less about hitting a specific 'ideal' number and more about ensuring natural and contextually appropriate use.

Utilizing semantic variations and synonyms of the target keywords enriches the content and aligns with modern search engines' abilities to better understand context and intent. This not only makes the content more engaging but also broadens its reach.

Page Meta Tags

Meta tags are snippets of text that describe a page's content and allow search engines to understand the context of these pages clearly. While they don't appear on the page itself, they are embedded in its HTML code. These are the tiles and descriptions that do appear on search engine results pages.

These consist of two main parts:

1. Meta Title Tag: The meta title tag should accurately and concisely describe the page's content. For effective SEO, relevant keywords should also be included near the beginning. The title tag is served in search engine results as the main clickable headline, telling search engines and users precisely what the entire page is about.

2. Meta Description: This tag summarizes the page content and is displayed in search results under the title. While meta descriptions don't directly influence search rankings, they do affect the page's CTR. A well-crafted meta description should be compelling, contain relevant keywords, and convince users to click through to the website.

Writing Effective Meta Tags

When crafting meta tags, adhere to these best practices to maximize their effectiveness:

1. Conciseness and Clarity: Keep title tags under 60 characters and meta descriptions under 160 characters - which are the current character limits in Google search. Both should be clear and concise.

2. Incorporate Target Keywords: Include relevant keywords in the title tag and meta description. For the title tag, place the most important keywords near the beginning.

3. Unique for Each Page: Each page on the website should have a unique title and meta description. This helps search engines understand the content and context of each page.

4. Reflect the Page's Content: Ensure the meta tags accurately reflect the page's content. Misleading tags can lead to high bounce rates as users may not find what they seek.

5. Encourage Clicks: The meta description should act as a 'sales pitch' for the page. It should be engaging and motivate users to click through to the site.

6. Avoid Overstuffing Keywords: While keywords are important, avoid stuffing meta tags with them. This practice is spammy and will turn off potential visitors.

7. Use Branding Wisely: If space allows, include the brand name in the title tag, preferably at the end. This can enhance brand recognition and trust.

Example:

https://thekingofsearch.com/

SEO Services | PPC | Inbound Marketing | The King of Search

We provide full-stack search marketing services, combining experience and expertise to help you achieve your business growth goals.

While they seem like small details, effectively written title tags and meta descriptions significantly impact your rankings for specific terms and CTRs in search results by users.

URL Optimization

The URL is often one of the first elements that search engines and users notice about a site in search results. SEO-friendly URLs are clear, concise, and descriptive, making them essential for user experience and SEO. A well-structured URL provides both users and search engines with a clear indication of what the page is about.

For users, a URL that is easy to read and understand can increase understanding, trust, and CTRs. For search engines, a clean and descriptive URL can be a strong indicator of the content on the page, aiding in better indexing and ranking. A well-optimized URL structure can also enhance a site's navigability, making it more user-friendly and ensuring a smoother browsing experience.

Crafting an effective URL structure involves:

1. **Simplicity and Clarity**: Keep URLs as simple as possible. Avoid long and convoluted URLs, which can confuse users and search engines. A simple, clear URL structure will likely be remembered and accurately indexed.

2. **Use of Hyphens to Separate Words**: Use hyphens rather than underscores or spaces to separate words in a URL. Hyphens are universally recognized by search engines as word separators, making your URLs more manageable to read and process.

3. **Lowercase Letters**: Stick to lowercase letters in the URLs. This practice avoids confusion, as URLs are case-sensitive in some servers, leading to potential issues with accessibility or duplicate content.

4. **Short and Descriptive**: URLs should be concise yet descriptive enough to give users a clear idea of the page content. Avoid unnecessary words or parameters that do not contribute to the user's understanding.

5. Avoiding Excessive Parameters: Whenever possible, minimize the use of URL parameters as they can make URLs lengthy and less user-friendly. If parameters are necessary, ensure they are clear and indicative of their function.

Incorporating keywords into URLs is another effective SEO strategy. Including relevant keywords in a URL can enhance its relevance and visibility in search results. However, it's essential to integrate these keywords naturally and avoid overstuffing. The inclusion should feel organic and directly related to the page content.

Important: Always be sure to implement 301 redirects when altering URLs.

Image Optimization

Optimized images enhance accessibility for users who rely on screen readers, as these tools use the image's metadata to describe the image. Image optimization also helps search engines understand what an image is about. Well-optimized images can also contribute to the overall SEO of the page they are on, providing context and supporting the textual content.

ALT Tag: ALT tags, short for alternative text, provide a text alternative for search engines and screen readers. Each image on the site should have an ALT tag that accurately and succinctly describes what the image is about, incorporating relevant keywords where appropriate.

The ALT tag is integrated into the HTML source code that displays the image. The primary goal of the ALT text should be to describe the image in a way that improves understanding for users who can't see the image.

Avoid stuffing it with keywords, which will be perceived as spammy.

Title Tag: Image Title Tags, often called "title attributes," offer supplementary information about an image when a user hovers over it with their mouse. They serve as additional context or clarification for both users and search engines.

Each image on a website should be equipped with a Title Tag that concisely summarizes the image's content, enhancing user experience, and aiding in SEO strategies by including pertinent keywords. Unlike ALT tags, Title Tags are not essential for accessibility but contribute to better user engagement and understanding.

File Naming Conventions: Before uploading images to a site, it's important to give them descriptive file names. A descriptive, well-chosen file name can provide context to an image and improve its chances of ranking in image search results.

Use plain language and hyphens to separate words in your file names. For instance, instead of naming a file "IMG_12345.jpg," name it "homemade-chocolate-chip-cookies.jpg" if it depicts homemade cookies.

An example image HTML code with these attributes:

```
<img loading="lazy" decoding="async"
width="300" height="300" src="/wp-
content/uploads/2024/01/brand-roi.png" alt="A
graph showing how increased brand presence in
search can positively affect ROI year over
year" title="Brand Presence in Search & ROI">
```

Internal Linking

Internal linking (deep-linking or interlinking), an often overlooked aspect of on-page SEO, builds a strong foundation for a website. It involves linking one website page to another page within the same domain. This practice aids in website navigation, defines the architecture and hierarchy of the site, and distributes 'link equity' across the site.

Link equity' refers to the SEO value passed from one page to another. Pages with a high number of backlinks have more link equity, which can be shared with other pages on a site through internal links. This distribution can boost the SEO performance of less prominent pages.

Internal linking also enhances the user experience, providing relevant links that help users quickly find additional information, increasing their engagement and time spent on the site.

Effective internal linking starts with a thoughtful strategy. It's important to create a network of links that feel natural and beneficial to the user. For instance, if a landing page lists a site's services, you could internally link each service name to a subpage, describing each particular service in detail. This not only aids in navigation but also establishes a thematic relationship between pages.

The anchor text, the clickable text in a hyperlink, should be relevant to the page you're linking to and give users and search engines an idea of what the page is about. Using natural, descriptive phrases for anchor texts rather than generic terms like "click here" (...Guilty.) is best.

When optimizing anchor text, it's important to avoid over-optimization. Repeatedly using the exact match keyword as anchor text for many links can appear manipulative to search engines. Instead, opt for varied, naturally incorporated anchor text that aligns with the context of each link.

Chapter 5:
Content Creation

Content creation outside of main website pages, in areas such as blogs or article repositories, is your key to crafting personalized messages for the many personas within your ideal user base, showcasing industry knowledge, and building a brand with a user-first focus.

Content writing is a discipline that blends creativity with strategy. At its essence, it's the crafting of text to inform and engage – and often, to persuade – an online audience. It is an essential component in building brand authority and credibility.

It requires an understanding of language, a sense of audience needs, and the ability to convey complex ideas clearly and compellingly. In an era where consumers are inundated with choices, the quality of your content can set you apart, transforming a website from a mere storefront into a trusted resource.

This is often easier said than done.

Well-crafted content speaks volumes about the brand's expertise and commitment to providing value, fostering a sense of trust that is the cornerstone of customer loyalty.

Content must be not only informative and engaging but also optimized for search engines to ensure visibility. This optimization involves a delicate balance, weaving keywords seamlessly into narratives without compromising the natural flow and readability.

The true measure of content writing's efficacy lies in its ability to convert readers into customers. Here, the skillful interplay of persuasive language, compelling storytelling, and strategic structuring comes to the fore. Content should capture attention and guide the reader toward a desired action. This journey from reader to customer is nuanced, requiring content that addresses various stages of the buyer's journey – from awareness and consideration to decision-making.

Content writing demands a synthesis of creativity and strategy, an alignment of business objectives with audience needs, and a continuous process of adaptation and refinement. At its heart, it is about forging connections – using words to bridge the gap between the brand and its audience, turning visitors into loyal customers and clicks into conversions.

Understanding The Audience

Gaining insight into the target audience means delving deep into this target group's psyche, preferences, and behaviors. This process demands more than a superficial glance at demographic data; it requires an empathetic approach that seeks to understand this audience's underlying motivations, challenges, and aspirations.

Creating a detailed persona of the ideal customer is where this all starts. The persona should encompass everything from job roles and lifestyle to online browsing habits and content preferences. A persona is a semi-fictional representation of a target audience based on market research and actual data about existing customers.

Here's a step-by-step guide to crafting these profiles:

1. **Collect and Analyze Data**: Gather data from the current customer base. This includes demographic information (age, location, gender), psychographic data (interests, values, lifestyle), and behavioral patterns. To compile this data, use tools like customer surveys, website analytics, and social media insights.

2. **Identify Customer Goals and Challenges**: Understand what drives customers. What are their primary goals? What challenges do they face in achieving these goals?

3. **Create Detailed Persona Profiles**: Using the gathered data, start building your personas. Give them names to humanize them. For each persona, include their background (job, career path), demographics, identifiers (communication preferences, demeanor), goals, challenges, and how your product can help.

4. **Include Real Quotes and Stories**: Incorporate quotes from customer interviews or surveys if possible. These add authenticity to your personas and help you and your team empathize with them.

5. **Revise and Update Regularly**: As a business grows and the market changes, so should its personas. Regularly update them to ensure they remain relevant.

6. **Create Scenarios and Pain Points**: For each persona, outline specific scenarios or situations they might find themselves in, along with their pain points in these scenarios. This helps in crafting more targeted messaging.

7. **Map the Customer Journey**: For each persona, map out a typical customer journey, highlighting touchpoints where they interact with the brand. This helps in understanding the best times and ways to engage them.

By creating and utilizing detailed buyer personas, you ensure that you improve the efficiency of your content efforts and enhance the overall customer experience, as your audience receives messages that feel personally crafted for them.

Here are some example profiles geared toward the audience for this book:

Persona 1: Marketing Maverick Mike

- **Background**: Mike is a mid-level marketing manager at a small to mid-sized tech company. He has a degree in marketing and has been working in the field for over five years. Mike is ambitious and always looking to improve his skills and knowledge.
- **Demographics**: Male, 30 years old, lives in a metropolitan area, single.
- **Identifiers**: Prefers email communication, active on LinkedIn, analytical mindset, enjoys reading and attending marketing webinars.
- **Goals**: Wants to enhance his company's online visibility and lead generation without increasing the ad spend significantly.
- **Challenges**: Struggles with limited resources and budget for big marketing campaigns. Needs to improve his knowledge of SEO to build a sustainable organic presence online.
- **How Your Product Can Help**: The book provides actionable strategies and insights into organic search marketing that Mike can implement immediately, even with a tight budget.
- **Real Quotes**: "I need to get our company's site to the top of Google without breaking the bank."
- **Scenarios and Pain Points**: Mike is frustrated with the rising costs of pay-per-click advertising and seeks long-term solutions to improve organic reach and ranking.

Persona 2: Entrepreneurial Emma

- **Background**: Emma is the founder of a start-up in the health and wellness sector. She is passionate about her business and has a strong vision but lacks in-depth marketing knowledge.
- **Demographics**: Female, 35 years old, lives in the suburbs, married with one child.
- **Identifiers**: Prefers direct messages and texts, active on Instagram and Facebook, creative, seeks efficiency, and values straightforward, actionable advice.
- **Goals**: Needs to increase her website's traffic and customer base through organic search to support her business's growth.
- **Challenges**: Overwhelmed by the complexity of SEO and digital marketing. Struggles to find time to learn and apply new strategies while managing her business.
- **How Your Product Can Help**: The book breaks down organic search marketing into understandable and manageable steps specifically for entrepreneurs with limited marketing experience.
- **Real Quotes**: "I know I need to get into SEO, but I don't know where to start and don't have time to become an expert."
- **Scenarios and Pain Points**: Emma is challenged by the need to balance business management with learning and implementing effective SEO strategies to grow her online presence and customer base.

Persona 3: Freelancer Fiona

- **Background**: Fiona has been working as a freelance content creator for the past two years, primarily focusing on writing blog posts and managing social media for small businesses. She has basic knowledge of SEO practices from her writing experience but wants to transition into offering full-scale SEO services to diversify her income and enhance her marketability.

- **Demographics**: Female, 28 years old, lives in a coastal city, single.
- **Identifiers**: Prefers text and email for communication, active on Twitter and LinkedIn, self-motivated learner, often participates in online forums and groups related to digital marketing.
- **Goals**: Aims to become a well-regarded SEO specialist in the freelance market, offering comprehensive SEO strategies and solutions to small and medium-sized businesses.
- **Challenges**: Lacks advanced SEO knowledge and experience, finding it challenging to compete with established SEO professionals. Needs to balance time between learning advanced SEO, delivering current projects, and marketing her new services.
- **How Your Product Can Help**: The book delivers comprehensive strategies on integrating content creation with SEO to achieve superior search engine rankings. It offers Fiona practical, step-by-step guidance on crafting content that resonates with both audiences and search engines. This resource will enable Fiona to not only refine her content creation skills but also to understand the nuances of SEO-driven content strategy, thereby enhancing her value proposition to potential clients.
- **Real Quotes**: "I know the basics of SEO, but I need to up my game to provide more value to my clients and stand out in the freelance market."
- **Scenarios and Pain Points**: Fiona is frequently encountering clients who require more advanced SEO than she currently offers. She is eager to learn and apply more sophisticated strategies but is uncertain where to find reliable, actionable information that translates into immediate value for her clients and her portfolio.

Why is this depth of understanding critical? Because, at its core, effective content writing is not about broadcasting a message into the void but about crafting a narrative that resonates with specific individuals.

The more precise your understanding of this audience, the more targeted and impactful your content can be. It's about speaking directly to their needs, addressing their pain points, and offering tailor-made solutions. This alignment captivates and builds a more profound connection, turning casual readers into engaged followers and loyal customers. It also positions the site as an authority in that particular domain, enhancing the trust and credibility of the brand.

So many websites across all industries ignore this that it becomes the magic bullet when implemented in most cases. It's about adapting your tone, style, and content format to align with the preferences of the niche audience. This could mean adopting a more technical language for professional audiences or opting for a conversational tone for community-focused niches.

The objective is to craft tailor-made content that reflects your target audience's unique interests and needs. Your content writing gains direction and focus and becomes a powerful tool in establishing a strong, resonant presence.

Demographics and Psychographics

Identifying the target audience begins with gathering demographic data, a fundamental step in understanding who the customers are. This includes age, gender, location, income level, education, and occupation. Such data can be collected through various means, including market research surveys, social media analytics, and customer database analysis. This demographic information lays the groundwork for market segmenting and tailoring content efforts to specific groups.

While demographics tell you who your customers are, psychographics reveal *why they buy.* This includes understanding their interests, values, attitudes, lifestyle, and personality traits. Psychographic data can be gathered through customer feedback, social media engagement analysis, and lifestyle surveys. By analyzing this data, content writers can comprehend the motivations behind consumer behavior, enabling them to craft messages that resonate on a more personal level.

This combination of demographic and psychographic data creates a solid base for developing targeted and compelling content campaigns that speak directly to the heart of the audience's needs and desires.

Behavioral Patterns and Pain Points

Understanding customer behavioral patterns involves analyzing how consumers interact with various touchpoints in their journey, such as website visits, purchase histories, and social media interactions.

Tools like Google Analytics, alongside social media insights, provide valuable data on consumer behavior, including the most visited pages, time on the site, and the content that garners the most engagement. This data helps identify patterns, such as the most preferred product categories or when consumers are most active online. Understanding these patterns enables writers to time content effectively and highlight products or services that align with consumer interests.

Pain points are specific problems that prospective customers of a business are experiencing. These can be identified through customer feedback, online reviews, and support queries. For instance, if many customers mention difficulties in finding a particular type of solution, this indicates a pain point that can be addressed in content. Addressing these pain points in your content establishes a direct rapport with the audience, demonstrating your understanding of their needs and your ability to fulfill them. This approach enhances relevance and builds trust and loyalty among the target audience.

Crafting Engaging and Persuasive Content

Going deeper into the art of content creation, let's explore strategies that can elevate your content from good to unforgettable.

Begin with a captivating hook – a compelling question, a surprising fact, or a relatable anecdote. This initial engagement draws the reader in and sets the tone for the rest of the content. The art of persuasive writing lies in subtly guiding the reader toward a desired action or viewpoint. Present arguments in a way that is both logical and emotionally appealing. Use clear and concise language to make your point. Back up your arguments with credible data, real-life examples, and expert opinions. This adds weight to your arguments and builds trust with the audience.

Techniques such as reciprocity (offering something valuable to get something in return), social proof (highlighting popularity or endorsements), and authority (demonstrating expertise) can be subtly woven into content to enhance its persuasive power.

When it comes to CTAs, clarity and relevance are key. A CTA should be clear in what it asks the reader to do and feel like a natural progression of the content. Tailor your CTAs to match the content – a blog post about health tips might end with a CTA to subscribe to more health advice, while a product review might conclude with a link to purchase the product.

Structuring Blog & Article Content

Structuring content for maximum impact and readability involves breaking down your content into digestible sections with clear subheadings. This makes the content easier to read and allows readers to scan through and pick out the most relevant information. Use short paragraphs, bullet points, and varied sentence lengths to keep the reader's attention.

A basic structural overview:

H1 Main Heading: The Core Topic of Your Content

Subheading: Key Aspect or Angle of the Main Topic

Introduction

- A brief overview of the topic.
- Engaging hook to draw readers in.

H2 Section 1: Exploring the First Major Point

H3 Subsection A: Detailed Aspect of the Major Point

- Key details or data.
- Relevant examples or case studies.

H3 Subsection B: Another Aspect of the Same Point

- Comparative analysis or contrasting viewpoints.
- Visuals or graphs to illustrate concepts.

H2 Section 2: Delving into the Second Major Point

H3 Subsection A: In-depth Exploration of the Point

- Interviews, quotes, or expert insights.
- Real-world applications and implications.

H3 Subsection B: Practical Applications

- Step-by-step guides or instructions.
- Tips, tricks, or best practices.

H2 Section 3: Addressing Additional Points or Perspectives

H3 Subsection A: Alternative Viewpoints or Counter-arguments

- A balanced discussion of different perspectives.
- Evidence-based rebuttals or confirmations.

H3 Subsection B: Extending the Discussion

- Broader implications or future trends.
- Call to action or concluding thoughts.

H2 Conclusion

- Summary
- Final thoughts and reflections.
- CTA

These structural elements help search engines understand and rank your content while improving the user experience for readers. Alongside this, incorporating elements like images, infographics, and videos will make your content more appealing. Visuals break the monotony of text, provide a break for the reader, and can be used to illustrate complex points more effectively.

The tone should align with the brand's personality and resonate with its audience. Whether it's formal, conversational, humorous, or inspirational, a consistent tone throughout your content helps build a connection with your readers.

Integrating Keywords

Integrating keywords into content writing begins with an understanding that SEO is not a separate entity but an integral part of the content creation process. It's about creating content that is inherently discoverable and accessible to search engines while still prioritizing the reader's experience. This integration involves a nuanced approach where SEO considerations guide but do not dictate content creation.

Utilizing the keywords you researched lies at the heart of this integration. Keyword optimization isn't just sprinkling terms throughout your content until some percentage is made up. You have to place them where they have the most impact strategically. This includes titles, headings, the first 100 words, and meta descriptions. However, the key is subtlety.

Keywords should fit into your content without being distracting, maintaining the natural flow and tone of your writing. Over-optimization can lead to content that feels forced or robotic, diminishing the reader's experience.

Internal and External Linking

When it comes to internal and external linking, this is yet another place where we will say to shut off that SEO tool telling you you need "1-2 external links" and "1-2 internal links." That's all garbage.

Internal links could go to a multitude of locations. We decide this by looking at them in a couple of simple ways. First, we want to be the definitive resource for the information we provide. So, if we find ourselves referencing some terminology or process we have already explained and don't want to repeat it - this is the first place we'll drop an internal link. This allows that user to dive quickly into a relevant tangent and offers us another area to showcase our knowledge in the space.

*if you don't have the resource, add it to your content calendar.

The next place we'll do it is when we want to pass equity to a page or pages we are trying to rank on the site. This must be done from a place of complete relevance within the piece of content but acts as one of the most potent forms of internal links you can provide for your target pages.

External links are where we place one hard and fast rule: The only external links to be sent out are those that reference content that is not in our wheelhouse.

(This rule applies to specific circumstances where we must adhere to Google's Your Money or Your Life (YMYL) rule. YMYL topics revolve around finances, safety, or health. Google only wants those who are trusted and proven leaders in those fields to be the source of that information.)

Most websites do not fall under YMYL expertise, so when we reference something in those fields, we will link to the *trusted resource* on which we are basing that particular piece of content.

An example is when we wrote a content piece about how much caffeine it would take to actually kill you.

This sounds odd, but we work with one of the strongest coffee companies on the planet, and this concern comes up in their social feeds all the time. We created that answer on the client site in an expansive article to give the client an easy answer that could be dropped in comment feeds. In that article, we referenced known reports and research papers from the National Institutes of Health (NIH), among others. We linked directly to supporting references in each area where we could not be the resource but needed to rely on these supporting facts and data.

This is the only circumstance that we will do it in. Everything else telling you to drop some magical number of links here or there is part of that SEO nonsense we are trying to remove from your world today.

How many links, though? Ask yourself:

- Well, how many references do I need to make?
- What is the benefit of this link for the user?
- Will this help rank another page?

If none of these fit, then you need none. If several fit, then you need several. There's simplicity in honesty. Don't get lost in outdated advice. Do what's logical. There is never a magic number of internal or outbound links you need.

Content Length

Content length is another matter of contention and has several correct answers. Content should be as long as it takes to provide an insightful answer. That rule will always work.

It is known that in-depth articles rank higher, but we've also seen two sentence-long entries in position #1 on Google. These nuances are rooted in the required depth needed for that subject, coupled with user engagement metrics. Which is really what we want to look at. What does the reader expect or need here? Meeting that expectation is the number one goal.

With that approach, engagement metrics go in the positive, which is really the final deciding factor when it comes time for Google to choose the final placement for a web page. I said "final placement" because we have all seen articles rank, be number one, and even hang there - and these could be long, very in-depth pieces that look deserving of the position. But then, after time, it starts slipping away. This could be from being outdated info or some other factors, but at the end of the day, it's almost always user engagement.

If you're coming in without data on how long a specific piece of content should be, do some detective work. Perform a few searches for your target, find the top five entries for each search, and start dissecting them for length. This will give you a safe starting point for any given subject.

Content Writing Tools and Resources

Today, content writers have access to an array of tools that aid in every aspect of the writing process, from research to final edits.

For research, tools like BuzzSumo and Google Trends offer valuable insights into trending topics, audience interests, and content performance across various niches. These tools help writers stay abreast of current trends and generate ideas that resonate with their target audience.

Tools like Grammarly and Hemingway Editor are widely used for their ability to detect and correct grammatical errors, suggest stylistic improvements, and enhance readability. While these tools are not infallible, they serve as helpful assistants in refining content and ensuring it adheres to higher standards of quality.

Content writers can benefit from websites like Coursera, Udemy, and LinkedIn Learning. They offer courses covering a wide range of topics, from basic writing skills to advanced digital marketing and SEO strategies. These platforms allow writers to expand their knowledge base, stay updated with industry trends, and continuously improve their craft.

Content writing forums and online communities (e.g., Reddit's r/writing or the *Writer's Digest* community) are valuable resources. They offer a platform for writers to share experiences, seek advice, and discuss trends. Engaging in these communities can provide writers new perspectives, inspiration, and valuable networking opportunities.

Podcasts and webinars focused on content writing, and marketing can be another resource for continual learning. They provide insights from industry experts and successful writers, offering practical tips and strategies that can be applied to one's writing practice.

Here's a list of some well-regarded podcasts and webinars in the content writing and marketing industry:

Podcasts

1. The Copywriter Club Podcast: Hosted by Kira Hug and Rob Marsh, this podcast dives into the ins and outs of copywriting, featuring interviews with expert copywriters and content marketers. It covers various topics, including freelance writing, marketing strategies, and writing tips.

2. Content Inc. with Joe Pulizzi: Joe Pulizzi, the founder of the Content Marketing Institute, shares his insights on content marketing strategies, how to build audiences, and ways to monetize content effectively.

3. Copyblogger FM: This podcast focuses on content marketing, copywriting, email marketing, and conversion optimization. It features interviews with content marketing professionals and provides actionable tips for content creators.

4. The Writer Files: Hosted by Kelton Reid, this podcast explores the habits, habitats, and brains of renowned writers. It provides insights into productivity, creativity, and writing processes that can inspire content writers.

5. Marketing Over Coffee: Hosted by John Wall and Christopher Penn, this podcast covers classic and new marketing strategies. It's an excellent resource for content writers looking to enhance their marketing knowledge.

Webinars

1. Content Marketing Institute Webinars: CMI offers a range of webinars covering various aspects of content marketing and writing. These webinars are led by industry experts and cover the latest trends and strategies in content marketing.

2. Copyblogger Webinars: Copyblogger has been a leader in offering valuable content writing and marketing advice. Their webinars often feature expert guests discussing topics like effective writing, content strategy, and digital marketing.

3. ProBlogger Webinars: Darren Rowse's ProBlogger offers blogging and content creation webinars. These sessions provide tips on writing engaging content, growing your audience, and monetizing your blog.

4. HubSpot Academy: Offers free courses and webinars on content marketing and writing. Their resources are excellent for those looking to understand the intersection of content writing and inbound marketing strategies.

These podcasts and webinars are ideal for anyone looking to improve their content writing skills or stay updated on the latest trends in content marketing.

Leveraging AI in Content Writing

AI in content creation is a double-edged sword. While it offers undeniable advantages, *over*-reliance on AI leads to significant pitfalls.

Tools like automated content generators, AI-driven research assistants, and language enhancement software are revolutionizing how content is produced, offering efficiency and scale previously unattainable.

AI tools can rapidly generate drafts, suggest content improvements, and provide data-driven insights, which can significantly expedite content creation. Automation in these areas allows content writers to focus more on strategy, creative direction, and fine-tuning content rather than excessive time on routine tasks. And, with capabilities such as semantic analysis and sentiment detection, AI tools can ensure that the content reads well and aligns with the desired tone and style.

However, one obvious concern about AI is the unavoidable loss of authenticity and originality. AI-generated content, while efficient, lacks the emotional depth (and nuance) that human writers bring to the table. It still struggles with context-specific subtleties and can fail to capture a brand's unique voice and personality.

Another limitation is the potential for ethical concerns, such as the risk of unintentional plagiarism or the creation of misleading content. As AI tools draw from existing online content to generate new material, there is a need for careful oversight to ensure originality and accuracy.

The most effective approach is to view AI as a tool that complements, rather than replaces, human input. It should be used to augment the creative process, not to automate it entirely. Writers should leverage AI for tasks like data gathering, language optimization, and content suggestions.

The core of the creative process – the development of unique ideas, emotional engagement, and brand-specific narratives – should remain firmly in the hands of human creators.

At its current stage, AI operates primarily by recognizing patterns and replicating existing data. While it can efficiently process and generate content based on these patterns, it lacks the inherent human qualities of creativity, empathy, and contextual understanding. This limitation becomes particularly apparent in tasks that require a deep understanding of nuanced human emotions, cultural subtleties, and creative storytelling. As a result, content overly reliant on AI can come across as formulaic, detached, and lacking in depth.

The risk of diminishing authenticity and originality in AI-assisted content is a significant concern. Authenticity in content writing involves expressing ideas uniquely, offering fresh perspectives, and establishing a genuine connection with the audience. If not carefully overseen, AI-generated content can lead to homogenization, where the content loses its unique flavor and becomes indistinguishable from the multitude of AI-generated texts flooding the internet right now. This not only affects audience engagement but can also erode a brand's identity and trustworthiness.

Effective human oversight and intervention involves actively monitoring AI-generated content for accuracy, relevance, and alignment with the brand's voice to mitigate these risks. This oversight also extends to ethical considerations, ensuring that the content upholds standards of integrity and avoids potential issues like plagiarism or factual inaccuracies.

To illustrate this danger, here is an actual excerpt from a piece of AI-generated content I stumbled upon online in 2023, published by a "lighting enthusiast" who claimed to have a bachelor's degree in electrical engineering:

Do You Have to Shut Off the Power to Change a Light Switch?

No, you do not have to shut off the power to change light switches. In fact, this is typically a dangerous practice that can result in electrical shock. If you are going to use your hands or feet to turn the switch on and off, it is recommended that you use an outlet cover instead. Changing a light switch can seem like a daunting task, but with these instructions, it's easy!

Individuals and organizations must implement thorough review processes to prevent issues like these. Strategies for effective intervention include incorporating an editorial process where human editors review and refine AI-generated content.

Besides fact-checking, this process should focus on enhancing the content's creativity, emotional resonance, and contextual relevance. Editors should add personal anecdotes, inject brand-specific humor, and ensure the content speaks to the audience's needs and interests.

Let's try applying this editorial process to the earlier bit of AI-generated content and see what happens:

Ever tackled changing a light switch and wondered, "Do I really need to cut the power?" Well, here's a bit of electrifying advice from my own misadventures. Once upon a time, I thought skipping the trip to the fuse box would save me time. (Spoiler alert: This was a shockingly bad idea—literally.)

I learned the hard way that electricity does not forgive, and neither does the jolt you get for underestimating it.

So, here's the deal: always, and I mean always, shut off the power before changing a light switch. It's a simple step that keeps you safe and keeps your hair from standing on end—even if that's the look you're going for.

And about using your feet to flick switches while you work? Let's leave acrobatics out of electrical work.

To effectively use AI in content writing, it's important to combine technology with human creativity. AI excels at data analysis and initial drafts, while humans add depth and emotion. Understanding AI's capabilities allows writers to use it wisely, maintaining content quality and authenticity. As AI technologies evolve, so will their applications in content writing; keeping up with AI advancements will help you stay competitive. Ultimately, the blend of AI and human effort can produce optimized, profoundly human content.

Crafting Effective Prompts

Crafting effective prompts helps harness AI's strengths while avoiding its pitfalls. It's about effectively communicating with AI tools to generate valuable content and maximize the benefits of AI in content writing.

The precision and clarity of your prompts directly influence the relevance and quality of the AI-generated content. Effective prompts should be detailed and specific, clearly outlining the topic, tone, style, and key points that need to be covered.

One effective strategy in using AI is to employ it for ideation and content outlines. AI can quickly generate a variety of content ideas and outlines based on your prompts. For instance, instead of a vague prompt like "*write a blog post about digital marketing,*" a more effective prompt would be:

"Give me 5 title ideas and a suggested outline for a 1500-word blog post on the latest trends in digital marketing, focusing on AI integration, with a distinguished yet relaxed professional tone suitable for a younger B2B audience."

Want to see how GPT-4 Responded to that?

ChatGPT:

Title Ideas:

1. "Navigating the New Normal: AI's Game-Changing Role in Digital Marketing"

2. "Beyond Buzzwords: Real-World AI Applications Transforming Digital Marketing"

3. "The AI Revolution: How Emerging Technologies are Shaping the Future of Marketing"

4. "From Data to Decisions: Leveraging AI for Smarter Digital Marketing Strategies"

5. "AI Unveiled: Cutting-Edge Trends Redefining Digital Marketing in 2024"

Suggested Outline:

Introduction (200 words)

- Briefly introduce the dynamic nature of digital marketing and the rise of artificial intelligence.

- Set the stage for the importance of AI integration in digital marketing strategies.

- Mention the target audience of young B2B professionals and the aim to provide them with actionable insights.

The AI Revolution in Digital Marketing (300 words)

- Overview of AI in the digital marketing landscape: Discuss the shift from traditional strategies to AI-driven approaches.

- Highlight the benefits of AI integration in digital marketing, such as enhanced customer insights, personalization, and efficiency.

- Present real-life examples or case studies showcasing the successful integration of AI in marketing strategies.

Emerging AI Trends Transforming Digital Marketing (300 words)

- Explore specific AI trends in digital marketing: predictive analytics, chatbots, voice search optimization, personalized content, and programmatic advertising.

- Discuss how these trends are being implemented and the potential they hold for transforming marketing strategies.

- Include statistics or studies to back up the trends and their effectiveness.

AI and Data Analytics: A Match Made in Marketing Heaven (300 words)

- Delve into the role of data analytics in empowering AI-driven marketing.

- Explain how AI algorithms use data to make informed marketing decisions and predictions.

- Discuss the importance of ethical data usage and privacy concerns in the context of AI.

Overcoming Challenges and Implementing AI in Your Strategy (300 words)

- Address common challenges businesses face when integrating AI into their marketing strategies, such as budget constraints, skill gaps, and resistance to change.

- Offer practical advice on overcoming these challenges and tips for successful AI implementation.

- Emphasize the importance of continuous learning and adaptation in the rapidly evolving field of digital marketing.

Conclusion (100 words)

- Summarize the key points covered in the post and the undeniable impact of AI on the future of digital marketing.

- Encourage young B2B professionals to embrace AI technologies and innovate their marketing strategies.

- Provide a call-to-action, encouraging readers to stay informed about AI advancements and consider how they can apply these innovations in their own digital marketing efforts.

OpenAI. (2024). *ChatGPT* (4) [Large language model]. https://chat.openai.com

This initial output can serve as a springboard for further development and refinement by human writers. It's a way to overcome writer's block or to explore different angles on a topic that might not have been immediately apparent.

AI tools are also adept at processing large volumes of data, conducting keyword research, and identifying trends and patterns in content performance. By leveraging AI for these analytical aspects, writers can gain insights that inform their content strategy and optimization, ensuring the content resonates with the audience and performs well in search engines.

The integration of AI in the revision process is also beneficial. AI tools can assist in grammar checking, read-ability analysis, and style enhancements. However, it's important to remember that human editors should review and approve these suggestions. The goal is to use AI to help refine the content, not to dictate the final product.

Establishing a process where AI-generated content is regularly reviewed, edited, and supplemented by human writers ensures a balance between efficiency and creativity. This collaborative approach allows for streamlining content production while maintaining the authenticity and emotional depth only human writers can provide.

In addition to these strategies, AI algorithms learn from the data they process. You can better train the AI to understand your specific requirements and style preferences by providing feedback on the AI-generated content. This ongoing training process gradually improves the AI's output, aligning it with the brand's voice and content goals.

Hiring and Working with Content Writers

Hiring content writers marks a transition from solitary content crafting to collaborative creation. Navigating the process of finding and hiring content writers begins with clearly understanding your content needs and goals.

Before starting the hiring process, define the scope of work, the desired expertise, and the tone and style of content you need. This clarity helps in targeting the right talent – writers who possess the technical skills and align with the brand's voice and ethos.

The search for content writers can take many forms, ranging from freelance platforms and professional networks to content writing agencies and referrals from industry contacts.

When evaluating potential writers, look for evidence of their versatility, adaptability, and ability to engage audiences. A writer's ability to understand and adapt to the brand's unique voice is as fundamental as their writing skills.

Once you have selected your writers, clear and concise communication sets the foundation for a successful collaboration. It involves outlining your expectations, providing detailed briefs, and setting clear deadlines. Effective communication also means being open to questions and providing timely feedback. This two-way communication ensures that the writers fully understand your objectives and can deliver content that meets your expectations.

Establishing guidelines should cover not just the stylistic and tonal aspects of the content but also practical elements like preferred content formats, SEO requirements, and any brand-specific dos and don'ts. Providing a comprehensive style guide can be immensely helpful, offering writers a reference point for the brand's preferred style - which ensures consistency across all content pieces.

Ensuring quality and consistency in outsourced content requires a system of regular review and feedback. Implement a review process where content is checked for grammar and style and alignment with the brand's messaging and goals.

Build a relationship with your content writers. Recognize their efforts, provide constructive feedback, and be open to their ideas and suggestions. A positive working relationship fosters loyalty and motivates writers to go the extra mile in creating content that truly resonates with the audience.

By navigating this process effectively, you can build a team of writers who are not just contractors but partners, contributing to the growth and success of your content marketing goals.

The Future Landscape of Content Writing

The landscape of content writing is not just evolving; it is undergoing daily transformations. The future of content writing is being shaped by technological advances and changing consumer behaviors.

AI's role is expected to expand beyond basic assistance to more sophisticated content generation and analytics, offering writers unprecedented tools for crafting and refining their work.

Another trend is the ever-growing importance of voice search and conversational content. As voice-activated assistants become more prevalent, content writers must adapt their strategies to optimize for voice search, focusing on natural language and question-based content that aligns with how people naturally speak and inquire.

The rise of immersive and interactive content is also reshaping the content writing landscape. Virtual and augmented reality technologies are opening new avenues for storytelling, enabling writers to create more engaging and experiential content. This trend calls for a blend of traditional writing skills with an understanding of these new technologies to create content that is not just read but experienced.

The future of content writing promises a landscape where creativity converges with technology and where content is more dynamic, personalized, and experiential.

Chapter 6:
Content Alignment
with the User Journey

This strategic framework is designed to engage potential customers at three critical stages: Initial Research, Consideration, and Final Conversion.

Each stage presents a distinct opportunity to connect, educate, and persuade, demanding content that resonates with the specific needs and mindset of the user at that moment.

Navigating the customer journey from initial curiosity to the final decision is no small feat. It requires a nuanced approach to content deployment, tailored to meet users where they are in their unique journey.

During the Initial Research phase, users seek information and explore their options without a definitive intent to purchase. Here, the focus is on providing educational content that informs and guides, establishing a foundation of trust and authority.

As users transition into the Consideration stage, they delve deeper, comparing options and evaluating the benefits of different solutions. The content strategy shifts accordingly, offering more detailed comparisons and expert insights that highlight the unique value proposition of the offerings.

Finally, at the <u>Final Conversion stage</u>, users are ready to decide. The content here is targeted, persuasive, and action-oriented, designed to alleviate last-minute concerns and encourage the user to take the final step.

This holistic approach ensures a seamless journey for the user, with content that addresses their evolving questions and concerns and builds a narrative that leads naturally to conversion. It's about being the right guide at the right time, offering the right information to move users confidently toward making a decision.

Focusing on User Needs

Creating content that hits right where it counts involves tapping into your target audience's unique tastes and pain points, especially when they're juggling many options.

Tailoring content to user needs is not just about addressing these points; it's about deeply understanding them and reflecting that understanding in every piece of content we create.

This understanding forms the backbone of creating user-journey-focused content that is unbiased, informative, and perfectly aligned with what the audience is seeking. Think of it as bespoke tailoring for content – it's got to fit like a glove every time.

The real artistry in content creation lies in translating the understanding of user needs into content that directly confronts and resolves the audience's pain points.

This delicate process of content crafting is where the genuine connection with the audience is forged.

But addressing pain points extends beyond mere clarification; it's about playing offense with your content. You're not just answering questions; you're preempting them. This isn't a shot in the dark; it's a strategic move based on a deep understanding of their typical concerns and challenges.

The content thus transforms into a proactive tool, offering solutions even before the audience has fully articulated their questions. This approach's crux is shifting from content that merely informs to content that actively solves problems. Each piece of content bridges the gap between user confusion and clarity between their problem and your solution.

This journey from identifying pain points to creating problem-solving content is not just about filling a website with information; it's about filling the audience's journey with solutions, ensuring that every interaction with content moves them closer to a resolution and, consequently, closer to the brand.

This process is not just about crafting content; it's about sculpting a unique experience for each audience segment, ensuring each piece resonates with them personally.

Think of your audience as more than just a monolithic crowd. They're a mosaic of varied interests, behaviors, and preferences. This diversity necessitates a strategy that transcends one-size-fits-all content. It's about segmenting this mosaic into individual tiles, each reflecting a distinct audience facet. Segmenting the audience based on specific behaviors and preferences paves the way for creating content that speaks directly to each group.

You need a solid feedback loop to perform this effectively and ensure you are on the right path. This loop acts as a continuous conversation between your efforts and the audience, where their interactions, preferences, and responses to the content allow you to fine-tune your strategy and guide you in your next steps. It's about listening through data, understanding through analytics, and refining your strategy based on this understanding.

This ongoing process ensures that the content remains relevant and deeply connected to the audience's evolving needs. By mastering this, you create a content strategy that attracts, captivates, and retains users, guiding them through their journey with information that aligns perfectly with their unique desires and requirements - in that moment.

Research-Level Content

At its core, research-level content represents the foundational layer of a content strategy. This content type is educational and informative and serves as your initial gateway for users in the early stages of their journey.

Unlike the consideration or decision-making stages, the research phase is characterized by exploration and information gathering. Users at this stage are not yet ready to buy; instead, they seek the knowledge to understand what solutions might exist for their needs or problems.

Research-level content can include comprehensive guides, detailed how-tos, thorough explanations of industry concepts, and in-depth explorations of topics pertinent to the brands' offer. Such content positions the website as a resource hub, attracting users seeking knowledge and understanding.

This approach ensures that your content meets the audience's informational needs, thereby enhancing engagement and building a foundation for a strong relationship.

To effectively address the audience's needs during the research phase, it's essential to understand what they are seeking. This understanding can be gained through various methods, such as market research, analysis of search trends, social listening, and direct customer feedback.

Each of these methods provides insights into the target audience's questions, concerns, and interests.

- Market research can reveal broader trends and preferences within the target market.

- Analyzing search trends helps understand the specific terms and topics the audience searches for online.

- Social listening gives a real-time view of what potential customers discuss and ask about in social media spaces.

- Direct customer feedback offers invaluable insights into the needs and preferences of the existing customer base, which can be extrapolated to understand potential customers.

This alignment not only improves the relevance of the content but also enhances the chances of that content being found through search engines, as it aligns with what users are actively seeking.

Initial Engagement and Brand Recall

When potential customers encounter high-quality, informative content during their initial research phase, it meets their immediate informational needs and begins the process of brand recognition and recall.

This content is often a consumer's first introduction to a brand, laying the groundwork for all future perceptions and interactions. By providing value upfront, without the immediate expectation of a sale, a brand positions itself as a helpful resource rather than just another vendor vying for attention.

This perception distinguishes the brand from its competitors. It elevates its status in the industry from a user perspective, making it more likely that users will turn to the brand when they transition from research to decision-making.

By addressing the questions, concerns, and interests of the target audience, research-level content also lays the groundwork for building a community around the brand.

Engaging with readers through comments, social media, and other interactive platforms can transform passive readers into active participants in a brand's ecosystem. This engagement further strengthens brand awareness, as engaged users are likelier to remember and recommend the brand to others.

Research-level content is more than just a means to inform; it's a powerful tool for initiating and nurturing brand awareness.

Integrating research-level content into the broader content strategy ensures that a brand remains relevant throughout the customer journey—from awareness through consideration and decision, and can even play a role in post-purchase engagement.

In search marketing, where information is both the currency and the commodity, leveraging research-level content to establish and enhance brand awareness is beneficial and a priority.

Research Level Content for Link Building

In SEO and search marketing, organic links are gold. Unlike paid links and those obtained through *link farms*, organic links are given voluntarily by other site owners or authors who find the content valuable enough to share with their audience or reference in content.

Paid link-building practices are often pitched as quick solutions to improve site rankings. However, these practices are less effective than organic link-building and are harmful to a site's long-term health. They also fail to provide the additional benefits organic links offer, such as targeted traffic and genuine audience engagement.

We consider buying links a downright waste of time at our agency. Organic link-building, achieved through creating high-level content, is inherently more sustainable and effective.

Search engines are constantly evolving their ability to identify (and penalize) sites that engage in manipulative link-building tactics. In contrast, links naturally earned through high-quality content are valued by search engines and contribute to the genuine authority of a website.

Creating content that naturally attracts backlinks starts with identifying the right topics. These topics should resonate with the target audience at the research stage and have the potential to be cited by others in the industry.

Here are some strategies for finding these topics:

- Analyze Industry Trends and Hot Topics: Stay abreast of current trends and hot topics in the target industry. Utilizing tools like Google Trends, industry forums, and social media can provide insights into what the audience and peers are currently interested in.

- Competitor Analysis: Look at what the competitors are doing successfully. Which of their content pieces are getting the most backlinks? While you should never copy content, understanding what works for others in the industry can spark ideas for your unique spin on popular topics.

- Keyword Research for Content Gaps: Use keyword research tools to find high-search, low-competition keywords. These represent content gaps in the industry that you can fill. Creating content around these keywords can attract backlinks, as you'll provide valuable information not readily available elsewhere.

- Leveraging User Questions: Platforms like Quora, Reddit, and even the comments section of relevant blogs and articles can be goldmines for content ideas. Look for common questions or problems people are asking about and create content that provides comprehensive answers.

The format and presentation of content can significantly enhance its linkability. Different formats can appeal to different target audience segments and encourage sharing and linking.

Consider the following formats:

- **Explainer and Definition Content:** "What is" and "Why is" articles are foundational pieces that demystify complex concepts within the business industry. By breaking down intricate topics into understandable segments, it is more likely to be cited as a reference by others writing in the same space.
- **Detailed Guides and How-To Articles:** In-depth guides and how-to articles that offer real value to readers are link magnets. They're often referenced by other content creators who want to provide their audience with detailed information on a topic.
- **Case Studies and Original Research:** Content that includes original research or case studies is unique and can position the site as an authority. Such content will likely attract backlinks because it provides new information that can't be found elsewhere.
- **Infographics:** Infographics are highly shareable and can simplify complex data or concepts. A well-designed infographic can be an effective tool for gaining backlinks, as they are often used to illustrate points in other people's content.

The key to creating link-worthy content is identifying topics with high link potential and choosing the suitable format to present that information. Combining valuable, in-depth content with engaging formats allows you to create resources that others in the industry will want to reference and link to.

Consideration Stage Content

The 'Consideration Stage' is where potential customers evaluate their options and decide which product or service best meets their needs. This marks the transition in users from research and brand awareness to decision-making. It is here where potential customers, already aware of their problem or need, start exploring the available solutions.

The content needs to be tailored to inform and resonate with the audience's specific needs and preferences, guiding them toward making an informed decision.

In the consideration stage, potential customers form preferences and shape their decisions. The content they consume here significantly influences their choices. This stage offers brands a prime opportunity to position their products or services as the best option for a particular need.

It addresses key questions: "Why is this product/service the best solution for me?" and "How does it compare to others?" This content aids potential customers in evaluating different solutions, nudging them toward a decision.

Content in this phase must be detailed, relevant, and crafted to address the audience's unique concerns and questions.

When it successfully hits these marks, it guides potential customers towards informed decisions and positions the brand favorably in their minds. By equipping potential customers with the necessary information and insights to weigh their options, brands can effectively steer them through this phase.

Decision-making guides are your secret weapon here. Think of them as a curated roadmap for potential customers, leading them through the jungle of choices straight to a decision they can bank on.

The art of creating these guides hinges on a trio of foundational principles:

1. Clarity: Clarity is the process of stripping away the complexities and presenting information in a manner that is effortlessly digestible. This means avoiding jargon, simplifying technical terms, and using language that speaks directly to the reader's level of understanding.

The goal is to illuminate, not to confuse.

2. Comprehensiveness: A decision-making guide must be comprehensive. From addressing the most common questions to comparing different options, the guide should leave no stone unturned.

This comprehensiveness ensures that the reader has a 360-degree view of the subject, equipped with all the information needed to make an informed choice.

3. Objectivity: While the underlying intent of these guides is to nudge the reader toward a product or service, objectivity cannot be compromised.

This principle is about balancing the scales, presenting facts and figures honestly, and offering fair comparisons, even if they include competitors. Objectivity allows the reader to make a choice that they feel is best for them.

This honest presentation builds trust and credibility, not just in the guide but for the brand as a whole. Together, these elements create guides that not only inform but empower the reader, guiding them through the consideration stage with clear, complete, and unbiased information.

The goal is to guide the reader towards a decision, not by pushing them but by holding their hand and leading them with the right mix of information and subtle persuasion.

At the heart of these guides is the principle of educating the reader. This approach transcends mere selling; it's about enriching the reader's understanding and knowledge about a topic or product. In other words, you're schooling them, not just selling to them.

When the content serves as a source of valuable information, the brand naturally positions itself as helpful and trustworthy. This perception is inherently persuasive.

Armed with knowledge and insights from this guide, the reader starts viewing the brand as an ally in their decision-making process. This builds a bridge of trust and gratitude. You're not just making a sale—you're making a fan. That's how you win this game.

Integrating Persuasion with Finesse

While the primary goal is to educate and drive a decision, weaving persuasive elements into this content mix must be subtle.

Elements like testimonials, success stories, or relevant data points act as nudges rather than shoves. They complement the information, providing real-world proof or backing up claims without overpowering the nature of the content. For instance, a testimonial can illustrate how a particular feature of a product solved a real customer's problem, making the information provided more relatable and tangible.

An often overlooked component of decision-making guides is the CTA. While the guide focuses on informing and persuading, the CTA invites the reader to take the next step. The CTA should emerge naturally from the flow of the content, feeling like the next logical step rather than an abrupt or forceful interruption.

It's about gently guiding the reader to the action you desire them to take, making it clear and accessible yet not overbearing. This approach ensures that the reader feels informed, not sold to, guided, and not pushed, resulting in an empowering and natural decision-making process.

Such content not only assists in the immediate decision but also builds a long-term relationship between the reader and the brand - ultimately leading to conversions.

Crafting Decision-Making Guides

The effectiveness of a decision-making guide hinges on its structure and clarity. A well-structured guide is one that categorically breaks down the information, making it digestible and easy to understand. It should break things down so even a kid could understand it.

The key here is to choose relevant criteria for comparison that matter to the target audience. These criteria should reflect the aspects users are most concerned about and the factors significantly impacting their decision-making process.

Utilizing visual aids like charts, graphs, or tables can immensely enhance the comprehensiveness and readability of comparison content. These visual elements aid in presenting complex data or feature comparisons in a more accessible and easily understandable format. The use of visuals breaks the monotony of text and allows readers to grasp the comparisons at a glance.

Keep it clear; keep it simple. You're not trying to impress with jargon—you're trying to communicate. Make sure *everyone* can grasp what you're saying regardless of expertise.

Place the coolest features and best aspects of what you're offering front and center, but keep it legit. This isn't about bending the truth or playing favorites. It's about strategic emphasis, highlighting where the product or service is killing it without twisting the narrative. Remember that your audience is sharp; they'll sniff out any hint of corporate slant or personal leanings in a heartbeat.

So, keep it 100% focused on the goals of the audience. Lay out the facts, features, and data with detachment, presenting each option in a balanced, no-BS way. In a world full of smoke and mirrors, providing clear, unbiased information isn't just good marketing; it's a power move.

You're not just selling; you're empowering them to make a choice they'll thank you for.

Conversion Stage Content

The journey from the Consideration to the Conversion Stage is marked by significant psychological and decision-making shifts in the buyer's mind. Here, the narrative of the buyer shifts from curiosity and evaluation to decision and action.

Unlike the awareness stage, where the focus is on introducing and informing the customer about a product or service, and the consideration stage, where the customer evaluates and compares options, the Conversion Stage is where the decision to act is finally made.

This change is often driven by a combination of factors such as perceived value, trust in the brand, and the effectiveness of the content in addressing any remaining uncertainties or questions. Marketers must understand these psychological shifts to guide the customer through this transition effectively.

This stage is characterized by a high intent to commit, where the customer has moved beyond exploring options and is now in a state of readiness to make a conversion. The content consumed during this phase is more detailed and specific, often including pricing information, detailed product specifications, or service-related details.

But let's be clear: conversion-focused content isn't just a shove toward the checkout. It's a strategic blend of persuasion, clear information, and solid reassurance. This content zeroes in on those last-minute hesitations, answers the final questions, and builds a bridge of trust and credibility.

This involves understanding common hesitations or questions that users at this stage might have and directly addressing them in the content.

For instance:

- If users are concerned about the quality of a product, detailed testimonials or case studies can be effective.
- If the price is a concern, content articulating long-term value and cost-effectiveness can be more persuasive.

This alignment helps overcome the last hurdles to conversion and reinforces the user's decision to choose this brand over others.

Main service or product pages on a website often serve as the destination point where the CTA in consideration stage content leads potential customers. At the same time, conversion stage content can be created in a blog or article area. This gives you a unique opportunity to craft messaging for each user persona you have identified.

These pages must provide a comprehensive and persuasive view of the product or service, encapsulating all the necessary information that a customer needs to move from consideration to purchase.

Strategically structured, every element is a calculated move in the game of persuasion. Text, visuals, layout—each component is a cog in a well-oiled conversion machine.

This means clear headings, concise and compelling descriptions, a prominent display of features and benefits, customer testimonials, and strong CTAs. High-quality images or videos that showcase the product or service in action can significantly enhance the page's effectiveness.

These pages should be optimized for ease of navigation and a seamless user experience, minimizing any barriers to conversion. They are not just informational endpoints but pivotal conversion tools meticulously designed to turn interest into commitment.

The effectiveness of this content hinges on several key elements:

- The content must clearly communicate the value proposition and the product or service's benefits. It should leave no room for ambiguity regarding the offer and how it addresses the customer's needs.
- A sense of urgency and relevance. This can be achieved through limited-time offers, showcasing a product's popularity, or highlighting a service's immediate benefits.
- The content must have a solid and straightforward call to action. The CTA acts as a guide, telling the user exactly what steps to take next.

This is where strategic creativity meets the practicality of sales-oriented communication. This is the core of conversion-centric content: striking the perfect balance between generating immediate sales and cementing the long-term relationship between a brand and its customers.

Principles of Creating Conversion-Driven Content

Clarity of message is a non-negotiable principle. In a system where attention is the hottest commodity, your content can't afford to be anything less than crystal clear. It involves distilling the essence of the product or service into a message that is easily digestible *and* resonates with the core needs and desires of the user. A precision-guided missile aimed straight at the heart of your customer's decision-making process.

The importance of clarity lies in its ability to quickly and efficiently communicate the value proposition of what's being offered. This clarity of messaging should permeate every aspect of the content, from the headline that hooks their attention to the detailed descriptions that provide depth and context.

It simplifies the user's journey by removing ambiguity and helping them understand how the offering aligns with their needs. It's showing them, in no uncertain terms, how what you're offering aligns seamlessly with what they need, want, and can't do without.

Use of Persuasive Elements

Persuasive elements in conversion-driven content are the subtle undercurrents that sway decision-making. But it's a tightrope walk.

Incorporating elements like social proof, urgency, and benefits-focused language can significantly enhance the persuasive power of the content. The key lies in striking a balance, ensuring that these elements enhance the message without overshadowing the authenticity and honesty of the content.

Social proof, such as customer testimonials or usage statistics, leverages the human tendency to follow the actions of others. It reassures potential customers that others have found value in the offering.

Creating a sense of urgency, either through limited-time offers or highlighting the popularity of a product, can motivate users to act quickly to avoid missing out.

Meanwhile, focusing on the benefits rather than just the features of a product or service aligns the content with the user's perspective, answering the crucial question, "What's in it for me?"

In all this, honesty is non-negotiable. Persuasive doesn't mean deceptive. The aim is to persuade, yes, but in a way that's as real as it is effective.

Strong CTA

A strong CTA is more than mere instruction; it's the culmination of your content's persuasive power, distilled into a clear directive that prompts the user to take the next step. Think of it as the closing argument in a trial, the final pitch in a game, the decisive moment where your content's persuasive power crystallizes into a clear, unmissable directive: **Act Now**.

A well-crafted CTA involves careful consideration of language, placement, and design to create an element that is both noticeable and compelling. The language of the CTA should evoke a sense of urgency and benefit, encouraging the user to act now. It should be direct and action-oriented, using verbs that prompt immediate response.

The CTA should be positioned in a way that feels like a natural progression from the content, appearing at the moment when the user is most convinced and ready to act.

"This is the next step, the action you need to take."

(FYI, It's to move to Chapter 7 in this case)

Chapter 7:
The Total Funnel Narrative Approach (TFNA)

This approach is a strategic amalgamation of content that speaks to each phase of the buyer's journey – research, consideration, and conversion – seamlessly integrated into one piece of content.

Alongside is the crafting of supporting and nuanced content that speaks to the target audience, builds authority, credibility, and trust.

The Total Funnel Narrative Approach (TFNA) represents a paradigm shift in content marketing, where comprehensive content pieces are meticulously crafted to cover the entire spectrum of the buyer's journey within a single narrative.

TFNA content serves as the foundation of a content strategy around which all other content orbits. It is a comprehensive content piece that addresses the evolving needs and questions of the buyer at every step of their journey.

Unlike traditional content strategies that treat the stages of Initial Research, Consideration, and Final Conversion as distinct and separate entities, the TFNA weaves them into a seamless continuum, offering the user a holistic and engaging experience.

By encapsulating the entire spectrum of the buyer's journey, from the spark of initial interest to the final decision-making process, TFNA aims not only to inform and educate but also to persuade and convert, all within a single narrative framework.

This integration ensures that each segment of the narrative is precisely tailored to meet the user's needs at that specific point, facilitating a natural progression from one stage to the next.

The approach maintains narrative coherence through meticulous crafting, ensuring smooth and logical transitions between stages, thereby keeping the reader engaged and moving forward.

Integrating the Buyer's Journey into a Single Narrative

TFNA creates a comprehensive content piece that serves as a one-stop informational and decision-making power-house for potential customers by weaving together the various stages of Initial Research, Consideration, and Final Conversion.

The methodology begins with laying the groundwork through research-level content. This foundation addresses the 'What,' 'Why,' and 'How' questions that potential customers have at the outset of their journey.

We establish a rapport with the reader by answering these initial inquiries, positioning our content as authorit-ative and trustworthy. Transitioning from Initial Research to Consideration, the narrative deepens to explore compara-tive analyses, expert insights, and detailed explorations of options. This shift is marked by a seamless progression facilitated by a narrative that anticipates the reader's evolving questions and needs.

Techniques such as thematic linkage, where topics introduced in the research phase are expanded upon in the consideration phase, ensure coherence and relevance throughout.

As the narrative approaches the Final Conversion stage, the tone and content shift towards decision-making. Here, the conversation turns to more persuasive, action-oriented messaging designed to address last-minute concerns and highlight the unique value proposition of the offering. The transition is crafted to feel natural and logical, culminating in a compelling CTA encouraging the reader to make an informed decision.

A necessary feature of TFNA content is the inclusion of on-page navigation, such as a table of contents (TOC), which allows readers to navigate directly to the area of content most relevant to their stage in the buyer's journey. This flexibility respects the reader's autonomy, providing a user-centric experience that enhances engagement and satisfaction.

Whether a reader is seeking introductory information or ready to make a purchase decision, they can easily find the section of content that meets their needs and continue their journey from there.

Personalization for Different Personas

Acknowledging the diversity of an audience, TFNA content is tailored to specific buyer personas, ensuring that each narrative resonates with its intended audience.

By crafting different versions of TFNA content focused on the same subject but geared towards distinct personas, we create personalized landing experiences that speak directly to each segment's unique concerns, preferences, and needs. This approach amplifies the relevance and effectiveness of the content, fostering a deeper connection with the audience.

By referencing established methodologies for creating personas, TFNA content pieces are developed with a clear understanding of the target audience, enabling us to address their specific pain points and aspirations with precision.

TFNA Content-Length

In crafting content under TFNA, we take on a task that requires meticulous research, iterative editing, and a deep understanding of our audience's needs.

The expansive nature of TFNA content pieces, ranging from 2,500 to 10,000+ words, reflects our commitment to covering every facet of the subject. This wide-ranging word count isn't arbitrary but is thoughtfully aligned with the subject's complexity and the industry's demands.

Given these narratives' substantial length and depth, on-page navigation—or a TOC—becomes an indispensable tool, guiding readers directly to the information they seek without unnecessary scrolling or frustration.

To contextualize the scale and intention behind TFNA content, consider the common experience of searching for a recipe online. It's a scenario many of us are familiar with: you're searching for a simple grilled cheese sandwich recipe. But you find yourself navigating through a lengthy narrative about the author's great-grandmother's adventures in Italy and her profound love for goats. While engaging, these sprawling stories, often followed by detailed discourses on the nuances of creating a grilled cheese sandwich, can frustrate users who simply want the recipe. While rich in storytelling, such content typically lacks user-oriented navigation, forcing readers to scroll endlessly past ads and unrelated anecdotes to reach the crux of their search.

This is where the TFNA diverges significantly from less user-centric approaches. While acknowledging the value of comprehensive, in-depth content, our strategy is fundamentally designed with the user's journey in mind. Every section of a TFNA piece is meticulously crafted to align with the searcher's needs, ensuring that the content delivered is relevant and easily accessible.

Implementing a TOC or similar navigational aids allows users to bypass content that may not be immediately relevant to them, offering a pathway to precisely what they're looking for, whether it's an overview, detailed analysis, or actionable insights.

Our philosophy centers on the belief that while depth and detail are valuable, they should not come at the expense of user experience. TFNA content is constructed to empower the reader, allowing them to explore content in a way that best suits their needs and preferences.

Each piece is a carefully orchestrated ensemble of information presented in a manner that respects the reader's time and intelligence. By prioritizing accessibility and relevance, we ensure that our content genuinely serves the interests and requirements of our audience, distinguishing our approach from the one-dimensional narratives that dominate many online experiences.

The length and structure of TFNA content are designed to reflect our deep engagement with the topic and our commitment to delivering a user-first experience.

Through strategic planning and thoughtful execution, we create content that is comprehensive, authoritative, and considerate of the reader, setting a new standard for content that truly resonates with its intended audience.

TFNA Content Structure

TFNA utilizes a meticulously structured format to enhance readability, navigation, and user engagement. This structure is characterized by the strategic use of header tags, creating a clear hierarchy of content that facilitates easy access through in-page navigation.

Each header serves as an anchor point, seamlessly integrated into the TOC, allowing readers to jump directly to sections of interest.

Example Breakdown of the TFNA Structure:

H1: Main Title

Introduction to the topic, setting the stage for the narrative.

TOC (Table of Contents)

A navigable list of sections, each linked to its corresponding header tag within the content.

H2: Initial Research Phase

Introduction to Initial Research

Brief overview of the phase and what readers can expect to learn.

H3: Understanding the Basics

Detailed exploration of fundamental concepts.

Visual Element: Infographic or video summarizing key points.

H3: Exploring Options

Comparative analysis or list of options available to the reader.

Visual Element: Comparative chart or slideshow.

H2: Consideration Stage

Introduction to Consideration

Overview of the stage, emphasizing the evaluation of options.

H3: Deep Dive into Features and Benefits

In-depth analysis of product/service features and benefits.

Visual Element: Video testimonials or detailed product images.

H3: Comparing Alternatives

Comparative analysis of the product/service against alternatives.

Visual Element: Side-by-side comparison images or interactive comparison tool.

H2: Final Conversion Stage

Introduction to Conversion

Explanation of the stage, focusing on making the final decision.

H3: Addressing Last-minute Concerns

FAQs or concerns with detailed answers to reassure readers.

Visual Element: Assurance video or certification badges.

H3: Why Choose Us

Persuasive argument presenting the unique value proposition.

Visual Element: Success stories or case study highlights.

H2: CTA

Direct Invitation

Encouraging the reader to take the next step, be it contacting for more information, signing up, or making a purchase.

Visual Element: Engaging CTA Button or Interactive Form

Positioned as a natural conclusion to the journey, inviting immediate action.

Throughout the TFNA structure, visual elements are strategically placed to complement the text and deepen engagement. These elements are aligned with content to provide a break from text-heavy sections, offer visual explanations, and present real-world applications of the concepts discussed.

The goal is to create a repeating cycle of engagement where textual content draws the reader in, and visual elements encourage further exploration of the subsequent text. The TFNA's structured approach to content creation offers a dynamic and interactive reading experience.

Combining detailed, stage-specific information with engaging visual elements and efficient navigation ensures that each piece of content delivers value to the reader, regardless of their position in the buyer's journey.

The TFNA Micro Funnel

The concept of a Micro Funnel within TFNA offers a sophisticated expansion of traditional content marketing strategies. This is similar to the relationship between a pillar article and its interlinked supporting content, content silos, conversion funnels, or topic cluster methodologies - but it is also none of them.

In the TFNA framework, this Micro Funnel model is refined and strategically deployed to support and enhance the main narrative's reach and effectiveness. A Micro Funnel consists of several shorter, supporting articles that delve into specific nuances or offshoot topics related to the main TFNA piece.

These articles are typically concise, ranging from 750 to 1,500 words, offering focused deep dives into areas that the broader TFNA piece might touch upon more generally. The goal of each supporting article is to explore a particular aspect in greater depth, providing additional value and insights to the reader.

One of the key features of the Micro Funnel structure is the strategic interlinking between the TFNA piece and its supporting articles. This interconnected web allows users to easily navigate from the main narrative to these detailed explorations and back again, creating a cohesive content ecosystem.

This seamless navigation ensures that users remain engaged within the TFNA ecosystem, enhancing their understanding and relationship with the content.

The Micro Funnel strategy is not just about enriching the user experience; it also plays a significant role in search engine rankings. By surrounding the main TFNA piece with a constellation of interlinked, topic-relevant supporting articles, the entire structure gains authority. This comprehensive coverage and interconnectivity help the TFNA piece, and its supporting articles rank higher in SERPs.

Alongside this, the authority of the main TFNA piece is shared with its supporting articles through their interlinks. This mutual reinforcement means that when users search for more niche or specific aspects of the main topic, search engines are more likely to present them with one of the supporting articles.

Once users land on these articles, they're seamlessly brought back into the broader narrative of the TFNA, closing the loop of the Micro Funnel.

The Micro Funnel within the TFNA framework represents a strategic, user-focused approach to content creation and depth. It leverages the strengths of traditional content marketing structures while introducing a level of depth, interconnectivity, and SEO optimization that sets it apart, ensuring that the content not only meets the audience's diverse needs but also achieves prominent visibility and authority online.

The TFNA Macro Funnel

The TFNA Macro Funnel represents a grand architecture of interlinked content ecosystems that comprehensively cover an entire domain or industry.

This advanced strategy involves the orchestration of multiple Micro Funnels, each dedicated to the different nuances of each buyer persona for each product or service the site offers. This tailored approach enhances relevance and conversion potential as users encounter content that speaks directly to their needs and preferences at scale.

Whether they enter through a Micro Funnel's supporting article or the main TFNA piece, users can navigate effortlessly across related topics, deepening their engagement and understanding of the subject matter.

The cumulative effect of implementing the TFNA Macro Funnel strategy is the transformation of the site into an unassailable authority within its niche.

This is achieved through several fundamental mechanisms:

- **Comprehensive Coverage:** The Macro Funnel's expansive scope ensures that virtually every aspect of the industry is covered, making the site a go-to resource for information seekers.
- **Organic Growth:** The interlinking of Micro Funnels within the larger Macro Funnel framework creates a network of SEO-friendly content. This lifts the site's overall search ranking, as search engines favor sites that provide comprehensive, logically interconnected content.
- **Building Trust and Credibility:** The depth, accuracy, and user-focused design of the TFNA Macro Funnel content build trust and credibility with users. Over time, as users consistently encounter and benefit from

the site's content, this trust translates into loyalty and advocacy, further amplifying the site's authority.

- **Endless Scalability:** The TFNA Macro Funnel's modular structure allows for endless expansion, enabling the site to adapt to emerging trends, new products, and evolving user interests. This adaptability ensures long-term relevance and dominance in search.

The TFNA Macro Funnel strategy represents a visionary content marketing and SEO approach. The strategy ensures unparalleled reach and engagement by creating a dense network of interlinked Micro Funnels, each addressing specific aspects of the industry and buyer personas.

Within the broader architecture of the TFNA Macro Funnel strategy, traditional content methodologies can play a role in enhancing and refining the overall approach. By integrating these conventional frameworks, marketers can leverage the strengths of each model to create a more robust and comprehensive content strategy. Some of these traditional content methodologies are content silos and topic clusters.

Content Silos refer to the organization of content around specific topics or themes without necessarily linking individual silo structures together. While this approach can lead to depth in individual subjects, integrating these silos within the TFNA framework can provide a more structured and interconnected user experience. Each silo can act as a standalone pillar within a Micro Funnel, contributing to the funnel's overall narrative and supporting the user's journey through targeted information.

Topic Clusters involve creating a series of related content pieces that are linked to a central 'pillar' post, which broadly covers a main topic. This method enhances SEO through semantic relevance and internal linking while building a larger and more comprehensive informational layer that contributes to deepening overall topical authority.

Marketers can create a dynamic and versatile content ecosystem by weaving traditional content methodologies into the TFNA Macro Funnel. This integrated approach not only respects the principles of traditional SEO and content marketing but also aligns them with a larger, more ambitious strategy. The result is a more comprehensive, user-centric, and search-optimized content framework that elevates the standard for industry-specific marketing.

TFNA Frequency

There's an art to getting the balance right between how much content you put out there and ensuring each piece is up to scratch.

Every piece of content that comes under the TFNA umbrella needs to hit the mark regarding value, accuracy, and engagement. This isn't just about filling up space on a site; it's about building brand reputation, cementing authority, and genuinely connecting with the audience. And let's not gloss over the importance of doing your homework. Thorough research and thoughtful content development take time and effort; this isn't the place to cut corners.

Whether you're crafting a keystone TFNA piece or a deep-dive article for one of your Micro Funnels, the goal is to ensure every piece of content is informative, meticulously researched, and perfectly tailored to what your audience is looking for.

So, while we're pushing the envelope on the amount of content and possibly ramping up the frequency of our efforts, remember that this is all in pursuit of a larger goal. It's not just about filling up your content calendar; it's about consistently delivering quality that speaks volumes about the brand and keeps the audience coming back for more.

Here's how to lock onto your content's target rhythm:

- Focus on your team. You need to match the pace of content production with their capacity. Pushing out content too hastily will compromise its quality.
- Monitoring what your competitors are doing is valuable recon, helping you determine if you need to accelerate your content cadence to stay ahead in the race. This is the top metric we use for initial pace decisions within industries.
- Engagement and feedback are like your applause meter here. If your posts get a lot of love, comments, and shares, it's a good sign your audience is asking for an encore.
- And then there's search placement—frequent, high-quality content deployments can help you break through, but it's important to avoid flooding your site with material that doesn't serve your strategic goals.

Each piece of content should be a strategic move on the chessboard, not just a move for the sake of moving.

TFNA Distribution

After successfully deploying a TFNA piece or one of its supporting pieces, we head straight to Google Search Console. At this point, we have an integrated sitemap. Odds are also high that we have a tool auto-updating that sitemap and a function to ping Search Console of the change. I don't care. I'm immediately telling Google to scrape and index those new URLs.

After that, it's straight off to social feeds. Whether immediate or scheduled, these will be shared on those platforms alongside their usual mix of social-focused, engaging posts. We'll leverage some other social link-sharing platforms, like Tumblr and Pinterest, and get them shared there.

After we know the content is indexed, *we may* syndicate that content on sites like Medium.

But one of our favorite things to do is hit Reddit and Quora. Because of the depth of these content pieces, we can almost always find someone asking a question that we have answered inside. When we find those, we have our profiles in place to naturally engage, give that answer in our own words, and say, "Here's a link that really breaks this down." Simple, effective, and unintrusive.

Then, we have newsletter flows. We'll integrate these content pieces as useful add-ons in newsletter campaigns. Because they are so insightful, they meet the user at any stage of their journey, and have expanded information that even current customers will find helpful - engagement goes immediately up.

If the business happens to be local and has a GBP (Google Business Profile), we will also utilize these as posts on that platform. To do this, we'll grab the cover or featured image for the post we created on the site and make it the image for the GBP post. We then create an interesting yet short description of the post in the text area and utilize the "Learn More" button option with the article link inserted. This offers another way to keep that platform updated and engaged without too much extra work.

With that little flow of events, we'll see traffic start flowing to these URLs, and we push the needle for faster organic growth simultaneously.

If the campaign fits, we add this as a site link or primary landing link inside a Google PPC campaign. We've actually seen great success running ads against these large TFNA pieces, leading to considerable conversion numbers. You can also leverage a cheaper alternative and gain some user insight and exposure simultaneously by running these through a Google Performance Max Campaign. Super cheap clicks that spread all over various platforms.

TFNA Link Building

Much like we brought up earlier, there isn't much to do here. I know all of these "gurus" and "growth hackers" in the SEO world will have a conniption over this, but that's okay.

Thankfully, we have never invested in a platform to "grow links" or banked our entire personalities on link building, and we get just to be honest and truthful here. These pieces, especially after some distribution effort, will absolutely grow organic and relevant links all on their own. We see it every single time.

I just monitored one that is about six months old with over 5700 backlinks. I started digging into those and found many niche-specific blogs referencing it, even several major news sites covering related topics referencing it. It's sort of insane to witness the first time, but it's always the result.

Chasing links is energy and oftentimes money that is best placed elsewhere- TFNA has you covered here.

TFNA Organic Growth

The really cool part is their organic growth potential. We do have to address the fact that the time it takes to come around varies for every specific case.

Sometimes, these happen as fast as the same day when part of a campaign that we have had going for some time, our subject authority has been established, and our engagement rates are incredibly high. Other times, it can be a brand-new site, and no matter what you do - it will take months to start seeing growth. That's just a fact until credibility is built up.

Competition within that subject will definitely play a role, but that's often where we hit the same subject repeatedly, with micro funnel after micro funnel. Again, the time is uncertain, but we'll get there. And we tend to get there fast because nobody else is hitting our depth or pace in most circles.

That aside, the outcomes are nothing short of impressive.

Due to the organization of a TFNA piece, these things not only rank for a multitude of target keywords around their core subject in search but we get featured snippet inclusion, "People Also Ask," "Thing to Know," "Where to Buy," image search, voice search - everything that is a SERP feature or tool, these things tickle the algo and get included.

That TOC we kept mentioning plays a role. Generally, under any of those search features, we can map it back to a linked section between the TOC and the featured content. It creates a little organization that makes it easier for Google to dissect and place these answers and snippets.

Remember when I said we'd reply to questions in Reddit and Quora earlier? With Google's "Discussions and forums" SERP feature, we create yet another place to showcase our brand in SERPs. Tip: Perform your target search first, see if this feature is present, and then go to those that are already visible and add your reply there.

This is how this content approach and structure finds everyone you are targeting, no matter their stage, and gets them right into your ecosystem. You dominate SERPs at every touch point within your target user base.

Increased Organic Traffic with PPC

The ultimate goal is to achieve a form of dominance on the search engine results page where a user's search showcases the brand in multiple formats.

We will dive deeper into Google Ads in another book, but the importance of having these run alongside your content campaign places pretty high.

We've discussed placement in organic results, knowledge panels, featured snippets, "People also ask" sections, and others. Still, alongside these, Google PPC ads can be the final puzzle piece to complete domination.

When you have a brand established at every stop point and touch point on a SERP within a single search, you are immediately signaling to that user you are the authority of whatever this search is. This multidimensional presence not only enhances visibility but also instantaneously establishes a funnel of brand recognition and trust.

We repeatedly watch where organic clicks go up in a search we are advertising against. And yes, we advertise against searches we are number one organically for. Initially, this was to keep competitors off the search and still is a facet of the reasoning, but also because of the increased clicks that happen alongside in organic results.

Whether it's a sublimable trigger from seeing the company name over and over or simply due to the complete infiltration in SERPs and the diversity of user choices regarding where they click, the result is the same: increased performance across the board.

When worked in tandem, this becomes a comprehensive strategy that leverages the strengths of both (paid and organic) approaches to create a dominant presence in search engines, ultimately leading to a significant increase in brand recognition, engagement, and successful conversions.

Chapter 8:
Analyze and Optimize

With monitoring and analytics, you peer into your users' minds, understand their intentions, and adapt to meet their needs - driving conversions.

The development and refinement of the TFNA rely heavily on analytics and user feedback. By monitoring engagement metrics, behavior patterns, and direct feedback, content creators can identify areas of the narrative that may require adjustment or enhancement.

This data-driven approach ensures the TFNAs remain relevant, effective, and closely aligned with the audience's needs, continually evolving based on empirical insights.

Google Analytics 4

Google Analytics 4 (GA4) is designed to collect and process a wealth of data about website traffic, offering granular insights into user behavior and content performance. These insights inform decisions about what content resonates with the audience and how to refine it for better engagement and conversion.

GA4 tracks and reports website traffic at its heart, but its capabilities extend far beyond mere traffic analysis. It provides a multi-dimensional view of visitor interactions on a website.

Understanding the intricacies of user behavior through GA4 involves a detailed examination of how user segments interact with the site's content, providing insights that can directly inform and improve content strategy.

By understanding and responding to these insights, content creators can fine-tune their approach, focusing on creating and promoting content that effectively meets the website's objectives and resonates with its audience.

Establish Measurable KPIs (Key Performance Indicators)

Regardless of the website's purpose, KPIs provide insights that inform strategies, drive growth, and elevate its online presence. You'll keep the business needs on track by consistently measuring and optimizing the right KPIs.

Here are some common KPIs. We often mix and match these to get a total picture of the website we are working with, alongside our goal sets in our tracking systems.

- **Conversion Rate:** The percentage of visitors who complete a desired action, such as making a purchase. A higher conversion rate indicates effective sales funnels.

- **Average Order Value (AOV):** The average amount a customer spends in a single transaction. Monitoring AOV helps maximize revenue per sale.

- **Shopping Cart Abandonment Rate:** The rate at which visitors add items to their cart but do not complete the purchase. A lower abandonment rate signifies a streamlined checkout process and competitive pricing.

- **Pageviews:** The total number of pages viewed by visitors. High page views typically suggest engaging content.

- **Bounce Rate:** The percentage of visitors who navigate away from the website after viewing only one page. Lower bounce rates indicate content relevance.
- **Time on Page:** The average time visitors spend on individual pages. Longer durations may imply content engagement.
- **Cost Per Lead (CPL):** The average cost of acquiring a single lead. Optimizing CPL ensures efficient budget utilization.

Advanced Segmentation

Segmentation is a powerful feature within Google Analytics that enables you to slice and dice data for deeper insights. Creating custom segments lets you focus on specific audience subsets and understand how different user groups interact with the website.

Common segments include:

- **New vs. Returning Users:** Understand how the website engages first-time visitors compared to loyal customers.
- **Traffic Sources:** Analyze the behavior of users arriving from various channels, such as organic search, paid ads, or social media.
- **Geographic Location:** Examine user behavior based on geographical location, helping you tailor content or marketing efforts.
- **Device Category:** Gain insights into user preferences and behaviors on desktop, mobile, and tablet devices.

Advanced analytics techniques are not about drowning in data but rather about using data to fuel informed decisions. They provide a deeper understanding of user behavior, enable you to optimize the website effectively, and uncover growth opportunities.

Flows We See With TNFA Funnel Systems

To give perspective on the type of activity we see when introducing a TNFA approach to a new client site in the first year, these are the patterns we always witness. To be clear, this excludes any paid (PPC) efforts and social, though many run all of this in tandem.

The first uptick is always *new users*. When we say uptick, this is usually leaps and bounds over the norm for the site. We'll witness this from organic in the first 90-day period. Conversions aren't *piling* in yet; this is the initial nurture stage, but conversions do begin to *trickle* in around this point.

At about the 6-month mark, we are seeing *steady* conversion events and can generally, at this point, prove growth in this month vs the same month the previous year. It's still not very exciting, but it makes sense for the client. Mainly because it scales steadily from here, and costs are being covered. The other thing that starts happening is that *return user* numbers begin to spike and break records for the site in this regard.

Then, between months 9 and 12, depending on circumstances in that particular competitive landscape, we get to the "*winning*" aspect of the entire process. *New users* are at all-time highs, and this never stops scaling. *Return users* are matching this pace. But now we see *direct visits* blow up.

At this point, we have nurtured leads, developed virtual relationships, and now folks are just coming straight to the source. As we proceed, *conversions* are happening at every user level: new, returning, and direct. It's the proverbial *snowball effect* displayed in data analytics and revenue numbers.

Now, imagine from day one, we are running PPC campaigns. This is where we gap-fill during the build phase.

And as the site grows bigger and bigger through content, that ever-important overall *relevance* factor comes into play. CPC (Cost Per Click) begins to reduce for the site fairly quickly through maximized quality scores. *Engagement rates* are through the roof, and we start having that SERP landing domination effect in full force at the tail-end of this timeline.

This is where our clients consider us partners, growth advisors, and integrate us for the long haul. I don't say that here for you to hire us; this isn't the point. The point is that whether doing this for yourself or building your own search marketing career - these are the expected and repeatable outcomes.

Integrating Insights from Search Console and Analytics

Merging insights from Google Search Console and Google Analytics transforms your approach to content strategy, offering a complete picture of performance. The integration starts with linking Google Search Console data to Google Analytics. This allows for the seamless flow of data between the two platforms.

Each tool has its individual strengths – Search Console shines in tracking website performance in search results, while Analytics provides a deep dive into visitor behavior on the site. Linking these tools bridges the gap between search visibility and user engagement data.

Google Search Console excels in providing detailed insights into how a site is performing in Google Search. Google Analytics complements this by offering in-depth information about user behavior once they arrive at the website.

By combining this data with information from Search Console, content creators can understand not only which pages are driving traffic but also how well this traffic engages with the site's content.

For example:

- A page may rank well for certain keywords and bring a substantial amount of traffic from search. However, if Google Analytics reveals that this traffic has a high bounce rate or low session duration, it suggests that while the content is visible, it may not be fully meeting the users' needs or expectations.

- Conversely, a page with lower search traffic but high engagement metrics might indicate highly relevant and engaging content that could benefit from improved SEO to increase visibility.

This integration aids in balancing SEO with user experience. While Search Console provides insights into optimizing for search engines, Google Analytics emphasizes optimizing for users.

Content needs to be not only discoverable but also engaging and valuable to the audience. Ultimately, the joint use of Search Console and Analytics empowers content creators with a dual-lens view, guiding them to optimize both the discovery and engagement aspects of their content.

Conversion Rate Optimization (CRO)

Conversion Rate Optimization (CRO)—it's not your typical stomping ground as a search marketer, but it's a territory you can't afford to ignore.

So, why do we venture into this territory? Simple. No matter how much traffic you generate or how laser-targeted your lead generation efforts are, it all falls short if the website isn't optimized for conversions.

Even if you're primarily focused on search marketing, mastering the art of CRO can be a game-changer.

While search marketers often find themselves building landing pages and working within the constraints of existing website themes and builders, understanding the fundamentals of CRO is key. It ensures that even if the entire site needs conversion optimization, the landing pages and critical conversion pathways you create are fine-tuned.

Much like web design, CRO is a multifaceted discipline in its own right. You might not be knee-deep in CRO strategies daily, but it's still a significant piece of the puzzle that can make or break your marketing efforts.

CRO is the systematic approach to transforming passive visitors into converting users. It takes the seeds planted by traffic generation and nurtured by design, ensuring they bear fruit in the form of conversions.

It involves a series of strategic changes and optimizations to various elements on the website, with the primary aim of encouraging more users to take those desired actions. It's a process of refinement where you analyze user behavior, identify barriers or friction points, and systematically eliminate or reduce them. This directly impacts a business's bottom line by amplifying the effectiveness of a website's traffic. Instead of just focusing on pulling in more visitors, you're increasing the chances of each one of those individual visits, resulting in the actions that matter most to your business goals.

Conversion rate is typically measured as the percentage of visitors who complete a specific action divided by the total number of visitors. For example, let's say an e-commerce website receives 10,000 visitors per month, and 2% of them convert (make a purchase). With targeted CRO improvements, the conversion rate could increase to 4%, effectively doubling sales without needing to double traffic.

This process involves improving the UX to steer users toward the desired actions subtly. It's about understanding your audience, their motivations, and their pain points and crafting an experience that aligns with their needs.

Common Pain Points

- **Slow-Loading Pages:** Users expect fast-loading websites. If pages are sluggish, users may abandon the site.
- **Confusing Navigation:** Complicated menus or unclear navigation paths can frustrate users. Ensure that the website's structure is intuitive.
- **Form Abandonment:** Long or complex forms can deter users from completing actions. Simplify forms and minimize required fields.
- **Unclear CTAs:** If users can't easily find the action you want them to take, they won't. Ensure your calls-to-action (CTAs) are prominent and clear.
- **Content Gaps:** They might leave if users can't find the information they're looking for. Identify content gaps and provide the information users need.

A/B Testing for Immediate Improved Performance

A/B testing is an experiment that compares two versions of a web element to determine which performs better regarding user engagement, conversions, or other prede-fined goals.

Every website is unique, and what works for one might not work for another. That's why A/B testing is a must. It allows you to experiment with different elements to see what resonates best with the audience.

Each element of the website serves as a variable. Through A/B testing, you'll systematically adjust these variables to discover what leads to higher conversions and a better user experience.

The list of key elements you should consider testing as part of the CRO strategy includes:

- **Headlines:** The wording, length, and tone of headlines can significantly impact user engagement and CTR.
- **Images and Media:** Different visuals, placement, and types (e.g., photographs, illustrations, videos) can affect user perception and interaction.

There's an *old-school* CRO trick with images where the person's face or eyes are looking at the next element you want the user to focus on. That element might be the CTA or even another element guiding them down the page (like an arrow) to where the CTA is. This still works - humans like to follow things.

- **CTA Buttons:** Button design, color, text, size, and placement can influence user actions, such as clicks or conversions.
- **Forms:** The length, fields, and design of forms can affect conversion rates, particularly in lead generation contexts.
- **Layout and Page Structure:** Adjusting a page's layout, organization, and structure can impact user navigation and engagement.
- **Pricing and Offers:** Testing different pricing strategies or promotional offers can directly impact sales and revenue.
- **Content Elements:** Elements like copywriting style, text length, and formatting can influence user comprehension and engagement.
- **Navigation Menus:** Changes in menu structure or navigation pathways can impact user journey and goal completion.

Being able to interpret A/B test results is a critical step in optimizing your website for higher conversions.

It involves more than just observing data; the approach ensures your decisions are based on concrete evidence rather than hunches or assumptions.

Here's how to effectively analyze and interpret A/B test results:

1. Measure Statistical Significance: Many A/B testing experts typically employ a significance level of 95%. This implies that in 19 out of 20 instances, the test results are not merely coincidental but hold statistical significance.

2. Consider Context: Examine the results within the context of a website's goals and its user behavior. A minor improvement can have a significant impact on user experience and conversions.

3. Apply Changes: Implement the winning variation as the new default on the website. *Ensure the changes still align with the web design and brand identity.*

4. Continuous Testing: A/B testing is an ongoing process. Continue to test and refine elements to optimize the website's performance further.

5. Document and Learn: Keep records of the A/B tests and their outcomes. Learn from both successes and failures to refine the CRO strategy over time.

By systematically testing and optimizing various elements, the website will resonate better with the audience and drive higher conversion rates.

Chapter 9:
Cohesion

In this book, we have delineated each component, method, and procedure necessary for effective organic search marketing.

Now, it's time to apply these concepts in a practical setting.

We organized this book to follow a logical sequence, reflecting the order in which we perform these processes. Along the way, we included the necessary context and knowledge to make each step clear and easy to understand.

The hard part is implementation; success lies in the nuances.

While we'd love to go through every type of business and apply these methods accordingly, that is beyond the scope of this (or any) book. Instead, we'll demonstrate these principles using a hypothetical business model that combines local and national services, e-commerce, and lead generation.

This approach allows us to cover the most common aspects you will encounter in a wide variety of projects. For the sake of this exercise, we'll assume we already know what the business objectives are, have all necessary access, and are ready to move forward.

Let's begin.

Initial Research

We always start with a quick visual overview of the website. Is it up to date with a decent design? Are there broken buttons or navigation items? Are we finding 404 pages? Does it display properly on various screen sizes? We can answer these questions pretty quickly with a brief inspection.

If we find that the site is so "out of whack" that we know sending leads there would be pointless, we stop everything and advise the client to address these issues with the web designer before proceeding.

But we'll say, for our hypothetical company, that all is good here.

From there, we immediately run the URL through two tools: one scan through SpyFu and one through SEMRush's Domain Overview Tool. Both of these tools tend to have variations in their data—current and historical search rankings, any hints of ad spend, and other intel. By layering both sets of data, we can create a composite view of the site's strengths, weaknesses, and overall performance.

On the organic search side, we start by looking at what the site ranks for on page one, what's on page two, and a quick scroll through the rest. This gives us a quick baseline in terms of the site's health in search. With the keyword lists from both tools, we first sort them by search volume, highest to lowest, and export that as an Excel file.

Then, we sort by competition scores, from easiest to hardest, and export a second file.

Next, we focus on transactional or conversion-focused terms—the big targets that can move the needle quickly. (We do need to talk about all three levels of users, including informational, but we're not there quite yet.) For now, we strip everything else out of the list.

We start here because we know the site is already on the radar for these, and focusing on them is the single fastest thing we can do to start returning money to the client.

We then look at the single biggest and most competitive term (or terms) the site needs to rank for and perform manual Google searches for them. We identify the top three competitors for each, analyze them with SpyFu and SEMRush, see what they rank for, export that list, and start sifting.

But maybe the site is not on the radar for many of the terms it needs, and we're not 100% sure the competitor sites are hitting all the marks. We'll now use some text tools to create mass lists.

If the site isn't on the radar for many of the terms it needs, and we're not 100% sure the competitor sites are hitting all the marks, we'll create mass keyword lists using text tools.

We generally leverage service names, location names, and product categories. (We don't go as granular as individual product names for large e-commerce stores— we'll get back to that later.) Then, we start mixing and matching all the variations we can think of with these assets and we create that list.

Notice we don't care about the search volume for these terms. Maybe some have it, maybe some don't—but all are relevant to the site and will act as overall health meters.

Once we've created the list, we set up a project in SEMRush and load the keywords into the Position Tracking tool.

We'll start with our list sorted by *ease of competition*. Even though the lists may all have these same terms, this is a method to insert and tag them without manually sifting through a massive list line by line. We'll load these first so we can easily tag them in the tracking tool. We'll use a tag for them like "Low Hanging Fruit."

We'll then get all off our other lists, combine them, remove repeats, and add them to tracking without tags. If there are repeats left, SEMRush will automatically exclude those.

Since our hypothetical company is both local and national, we'll create multiple tracking setups:

1. Google: United States - Desktop
2. Google: United States - Mobile
3. Google: Local Area - Desktop
4. Google: Local Area - Mobile
5. Bing: United States - Desktop
6. Bing: United States - Mobile
7. Bing: Local Area - Desktop
8. Bing: Local Area - Mobile

We'll then give these some time to populate with current positions and search volume data.

For simplicity, we won't get into SEMRush Listing Management here, but it's worth noting that it offers tools for tracking growth in Google Business rankings and citations. Those would typically be implemented at this stage as well.

That's it for now. We have enough data flowing to start the tracking portion of the campaign, and can move on to the site itself.

The Website

We tackle the website next because, often, we can make small tweaks that can lead to immediate gains—but we can only see that if we're already tracking the site's performance. Without tracking, you might inadvertently cause setbacks instead of improvements.

In our example scenario, the site is on WordPress, the most common platform. (Shopify and other CMS platforms have similar plugins and tools for optimization, so you can follow the same general flow.)

We are immediately installing RankMath in our project site. While we won't use all of its features, the ones we *do* use are some of the best available for WordPress optimization. During the setup process, the plugin asks for some basic information about the site.

Since this site operates both locally and nationally, we'll select the "local" option. This setting provides the most benefits overall. (Setting Local Schema won't negatively impact national rankings, but it will boost local perform-ance, which tends to be more challenging. We want all the cards in our favor here.)

We'll say "yes" to a sitemap, we'll say "yes" to opening all external links in a new tab, along with other relevant base options according to the project's needs.

Once the setup is complete, we head to the RankMath dashboard and disable everything we don't need. We shut off everything except:

- 404 Monitor
- Redirections
- ACF (if applicable)
- Image SEO
- Instant Indexing
- Local SEO
- Schema
- Sitemap
- WooCommerce (Since our site is e-commerce on WordPress, we'll assume they are using WooCommerce)

And that's it. We want nothing to do with the link counter, SEO analyzer, and definitely not Content AI. Don't fall for any of these things. Please.

Once we've set up the essentials, we go into each enabled feature in the RankMath dashboard and fine-tune all the available settings. Fill out everything that's relevant.

From here, you can make a move right now that can change a site for the better. Open that 404 monitor.

We find, time and time again, that sites get redesigned often, but they never 301 redirect old URLs to the new ones. This is always a heartbreaker for us. Web designers: if you implemented this step, you'd stop getting calls about how you destroyed their site in search. Seriously.

Especially with sites that are years and years old, have old social shares, old directories, have all that stuff they did in a forum back in the day, and everything else that can leave a little link trail around the internet—that 404 monitor will show you what they are, and frankly, the ones that still matter. If humans and crawlers are hitting those links and seeing 404s all day, there's your loss after the redesign. But not to fear—we are now in there, correcting these.

During the first 30 days, we monitor 404s closely. We figure out what each old URL may have meant, or originally led to, and create a 301 redirect to the most relevant page on the new site using RankMath's Redirections tool.

With that single move, bringing crawlers from far and wide back in the ecosystem, and all that link juice lying around back to this site, you'll usually see near-instant satisfaction. We have watched an extreme baseline push with immediate effect from this one task over and over again.

As a note, the 404 Monitor will also show all the bot spam/hack attempts. Use your judgment to ignore 404s that are obviously from these attempts.

These might look like:

- ws/info
- /logloadtime.php
- Public/home/js/check.js
- /static/admin/javascript/hetong.js
- m/_Fm7-alert.mp3

And so forth. After a while, you get used to these and learn just to ignore them completely.

We also generally don't bother with old image links, unless we find that it is causing a broken image on a live page.

Next, we head straight to the "All Pages" view in WordPress. It's common to find leftover "sample" pages or half-finished attempts at creating pages that are still live, even if they're not linked anywhere on the main site. If the site has an integrated sitemap, these dummy pages are being fed to Google, which isn't ideal. We clean these up by trashing them and setting 301 redirects if needed.

At this point, our SEMRush position tracking should have our baseline rankings settled. Now, we need to go in there and look at the various keywords that will make the biggest impact on this site. The hard stuff. The "We ain't gonna win this for a year" stuff. We'll make note of these and sift through the site again to find the pages that can best be aligned with them.

This brings us to the next move: Creating new pages.

For us, the first 30 days are all about this setup and optimization process. But we sell a content creation effort from day one.

When starting a project, we usually find the site missing detailed pages. For instance, there is a common implemen-tation of a "Services" page on websites that simply lists all services, but there is no deeper landing page for each service.

Not only will the site never rank for these; we have nothing to rank the site against without them. Our first content creation effort is making these missing pages—a *necessary* evil.

Using our knowledge of page design for conversion events and on-page optimization, we create a repeatable framework for these pages. This allows us to easily duplicate the page and "fill in the blanks" for the desired target.

In Elementor, for example, you can build a custom layout for a service page, and save it under My Templates so you can easily insert it in any new page.

Another method involves installing a page duplication plugin. Simply click "duplicate" in the WordPress pages area beneath the formatted page you wish to reuse. You'll need to edit the page URL for each duplicate, as the duplication process will add numbers to them.

Like:

– Original Page URL: /service-page/
– Duplicate Page 1 URL: /service-page-1/
– Duplicate Page 2 URL: /service-page-2/

We'll go ahead and clean those up with our target search terms:

– /i-am-this-service/
– /im-a-particular-service/
– /i-too-provide-service/

Once our pages are created and complete, we deep link (interlink) them from the main services page. We'll also typically create a dropdown menu under "Services," allowing users to navigate directly to the specific service they're interested in.

At this point, we've identified our targets, filled any obvious gaps, and need to ensure the site's front end reflects these objectives clearly.

Next, we perform an on-page sweep of all existing pages. We move page by page, making sure our headings—starting with the H1s—are targeted and logical. We then review the messaging on each page to see where we can implement some finer points to our targeting that match our overall search goals.

The homepage always gets assigned the hardest and biggest term target we need to win for the business.

Now that we have all of our pages in order, we'll go through and edit each one in the WordPress editor. (Not Elementor or whatever the site is using as a builder, the standard page editor.)

This is where RankMath becomes important again, offering one of the key functions we use: page metadata (RankMath > General). We will create headlines for our search targets and our initial ideas to improve user CTRs alongside click-worthy descriptions. We won't immediately know if we have these right; instead, we'll monitor their performance over time. Stay within the character and space limits so you can leverage all available real estate here.

Next, we switch to the "Social" tab in RankMath to refine titles, descriptions, and the social share image that appears in link previews on platforms like Facebook or X.

Don't be tempted to put in a "Target Keyword" here. You'll find yourself lost in that old-school ideology of keyword density percentages and all that other garbage that has zero effect on the site. If you're talking naturally about your primary keyword target on a given page, you have optimized the text on that page. Remember, you're speaking to humans, not a pre-programmed plugin.

Once this process is complete, we've hit another checkpoint. Next, we move on to more technical matters.

Speed, Search Console, and Analytics Review

Now that we have cleaned up the site, added pages as needed, and optimized them, we'll now look at site speed.

There would have been no point in doing this before making all the changes because we would need to do it again afterward to ensure we didn't inadvertently slow it down with our modifications. Whether you know you caused it or not is pointless - we're now going to fix any issue we find, regardless. We're all about streamlining our efforts, which saves time.

Now, most people focus on Google's PageSpeed Insights. It's an important tool that will tell you a lot, but don't get hung up on getting a perfect score here. Depending on the site's complexity and many other things, this almost always scores low - at best. Extremely simple sites with high-end static page caching services do well here. But when e-commerce is involved (as in our example site), we find this level of caching can trigger issues.

However, here, we are concerned with CLS (Cumulative Layout Shift). We want that in the green. This measurement refers to the web page's layout physically shifting while it's loading, which happens quite often with animated headlines or images. The goal here is to make sure the page isn't shifting elements so slowly that a user can accidentally click a button they didn't mean to click.

If CLS has a failing score, we almost always find it is from animated elements on the page. A few options here include removing the animations altogether, speeding the animation up, or disabling them on mobile devices only (if that's the only place it's actually failing).

Now, for user-facing website speed, we'll use a service like GTMetrix or Pingdom to see the actual load time. We are aiming for less than 3 seconds. If we find that we have a number around 3 seconds or less in these tools, generally, we won't be doing anything.

However, if you find the load time higher than this, you'll need to look down in the reports and see what is mentioned there. A lot of times, it has to do with images combined with server speed and caching issues.

We'll handle the images first. In WordPress and via some other tools available off-site, you can run the images in the media gallery through a plugin that reduces all of their file sizes. Some even change the image format to WebP, which is the current standard.

Now, those tools will reduce overall image file sizes across the board. However, we now need to examine all the elements on the slow page specifically. In particular, those images within small info boxes or similar elements.

Maybe the info box image is cropped to 300x300px in the live view, but the actual image being loaded is 1200x1200px. In these cases, you'll want to run those images through an image editor (we use Photoshop) and edit their size to fit the exact dimensions of the element they are in.

After we sweep through the images, we'll move to some of the other errors.

In general, a lot of the server-side response time and caching options are tools only accessible via the hosting provider's dashboard. This may be completely out of your wheelhouse, and all you can do is tell the site owner they need a faster hosting environment.

Sometimes that means adding some CDN (Content Delivery Network) service and additional caching upgrades. Other times it means finding a new host. Hosting providers like SiteGround and Kinsta are good options for WordPress sites, and they each have great support (which is very important).

You may also find plugins that resolve some speed issues. However, experience tells us that each one is quirky, and each one can have its own little conflicts with other items on the site. You can test these - there is a new one every day - but do make sure you're performing a full function check on the website after implementing them.

Essentially, at this point, we've done all we can do here, given our role in this project. If you've done everything you can do, and that site is still slow, it may be time for a heart-to-heart with the site owner.

Now, we've seen sites take as long as 7 or 8 seconds to load and still do fine overall in terms of engagement and conversions. But, these sites often leverage browser caching, so it is only slow for a user once.

You'll have to use your judgment here for a breaking point, but the site owner needs to know that you can no longer guarantee any of your work performing well with an issue like this. Keep trying to push them to upgrade their hosting and caching services - this solves speed issues 99% of the time.

Google Search Console (GSC)

Maintaining our order, we now head to GSC. We wait until now because, again, we've made all of our changes and optimizations, and we only now want to tell Google to come check it out.

Here, we will first go to the Sitemap area and make sure our sitemap URL is set there. If it is already set there, you're probably fine to move away. If there isn't one, go ahead and drop that URL there. Usually, the file URL will look something like sitemap.xml or sitemap_index.xml.

From here, we'll jump to the "Core Web Vitals" menu item and see what we see there.

In general, if you see any issue, odds are we have attempted to fix it by now. Open each line where a "Poor" rating is involved, see what it is, and go ahead and click that "Validate Fix" button to see where we settle out in the end. It may take Google a day or two to update your request.

Lastly, while we're in here, we'll take a peek at the Performance "Full Report" screen. We'll kick that back to a 16-month view and just take a scan at the ebbs and flows of traffic over time to get a general idea of how the site has been doing in Google search.

While in there, we'll also look at the "Queries," but keep in mind that this is far from an actual view of what is triggering searches for the site. You'll generally see this right away when we go to the next screen tab, "Pages", and note immediately that the top pages on this screen don't match most or sometimes any of the "Queries" on the first.

We do like to copy these top page URLs, paste them to a file, run back to SpyFu and SEMRush overview tools, and then study these exact URLs to see what they are ranking for. If we find they are ranking for relevant things that we don't have in our tracking yet, we'll go ahead and add these new keywords now.

You may find that some of these pages are close to ranking for bigger targets, and now you have some additional base pages to work with during the campaign. If they are already perfectly optimized from your purview, we will use them as deep-link targets in our content campaign to start pushing them up in search. With all of this in mind, we now know what your first topics will be.

Google Analytics (GA4)

In GA4, we are moving past technical issues and focusing solely on historical performance. We'll jump right to the Reports tab in the menu, and under whichever "Business Objectives" setting they have set, we'll open those and click "User Acquisition."

This is a report of all new users brought to the site.

Here, we'll view the data in a few ways:

- Past 30 days vs Previous 30 Days
- Past 30 Days vs Same Period Last Year (match day of week)
- Past 90 Days vs Same Period Last Year (match day of week)
- This Year vs Same Period Last Year (match day of week)

This is more of a mental exercise to get a grasp of what channels are driving traffic and then how that performs over various periods. We always like to study year vs year because that view accounts for seasonal swings.

Seasonal swings are important to understand because you may be in a project where everything starts nosediving, but in reality, it's not something you did. It's a temporary change in demand.

If you don't have year-over-year data to compare, the next best thing is to run over to Google Trends and perform some broad searches there for the main industry type you're working with.

Here, kick it back to a 5-year view, or all time, and start looking at the highs and lows. You'll almost always see a pattern. When you find that pattern, you now know that during x period of the year, we should expect losses, and during y period of the year, it should peak out.

Your goal is to take that year-over-year comparison in Analytics and prove growth this way. Trying always to show growth month to month (aside from keyword growth) isn't going to work in most cases. Instead, we want to say, "This June, compared to June of last year, we saw an increase in organic traffic of 45% and conversions of 35%." This is the best system of measure.

Those notes aside, from here, we'll run over to the "Examine Human Behavior" menu item and then click "Pages and Screens."

We'll kick this view back to 90 Days vs *Same Period Last Year (match day of week)*, study what pages have the most engagement now, see how that compared to those same pages last year, and make notes of any significant wins or losses.

In this same screen, we'll now click the comparison option next to the words "Page path and screen class" (the blue + icon). When that opens, we'll select Traffic Source > Cross Channel > Sessions Source and Medium.

We can now look at which platforms these users came from - which search engine, social feeds, referrals, etc. - and note how each platform performs for each page.

You may note that a page is absolutely killing it with Social or Paid Ads traffic but is utterly devoid of Organic traffic. In this situation, you know the page works; you just need to drive your primary source of traffic (organic search users) to it. Again, this type of information can inform you where you need to concentrate first in your main organic campaign.

Lead Gen

By this point, we have analyzed a lot of data, specifically pages that exhibit high user engagement across the site. Sometimes, these can be blog posts that existed before you came into the picture. Generally, we won't review the hundreds or thousands of blog posts a new client's site may have, except for those we have identified as performing well so far.

In any case, we now have some known entry points for users that perform well. We need to consider some CRO tactics for these pages.

Often, sites focused on lead generation will have a "quick" contact form on the home page, with all other CTAs directed to the Contact page. This is a system that works, but we want to eliminate any unnecessary steps that could hinder a conversion event.

Bearing this in mind, we will examine our list of high-performing pages and visually inspect each one. Do they have a clear CTA? Is the lead generation form or "click to call" button readily accessible? If not, we need to incorporate these elements, whether on a page or blog post.

In WordPress, we'll generally use a contact form system like Contact Form 7 (CF7) or Gravity Forms. These both have a shortcode function that you can copy and paste into any page or builder element. This allows you to integrate these forms where you need them easily.

If the "click to call" button is part of the strategy, provide both options right there. For this, we'll typically set up a two-column element on the page, placing the form on one side and the call button, along with some messaging, on the other.

The exact implementation of this integration depends on the builder and add-ons the site uses.

With something like Elementor, you could save this two-column element in your templates and then go to all your main site pages to add it efficiently across the site, wherever you think it's important.

Now, as far as tracking these events, things can get granular and heavily involved in their setup. We'll throw out some of the better options you can make use of next, but for simplicity, we'll finish up with something straightforward.

With contact forms, instead of repeatedly using the same one, you can keep duplicating that form. Even if all the fields and their destinations remain unchanged, you can add some visual tracking cues for both you and the client.

For example, we could modify the Subject Line field to say something like "Inquiry for *Service 1*" and place it on the *Service 1* page. Then, repeat this process for *Service 2*, *Service 3*, etc.

With this approach, we can create custom subject lines for all the main site pages, whether they are service-related or not. This way, we immediately know from which part of the site the inquiries came without having to crunch data.

Next, we integrate Google Tag Manager to track on-click events for form submissions on a per-page basis and then feed that conversion event data into GA4. This method allows you to easily track everything about the user's path to get there, which paths are performing best overall, and which ones need improvement—right within GA4. It's worth mentioning that these are then easily fed to the Google Ads platform through some built-in integration options so you can target these conversion events in your PPC efforts.

However, we are going to dumb this down to a simple, somewhat effective form of conversion tracking. First, Contact Form 7 does not come natively with an email log. You need to install a plugin called Flamingo, which records form submissions from CF7 on the site. Gravity Forms already has this integrated under Entries for each form.

Email logs are a great tool to see if emails are coming through (for yourself); then, you can cross-reference with the client to see if they are actually getting them. (That email log has saved my own butt a few times. Always check your spam folders!)

But the easy way to set up a form conversion event is to redirect the user to a *thank you* page after the submission. Again, CF7 does not offer this option natively, but there is an add-on plugin that will perform this function. Gravity Forms already has this option built in.

You'll need to create the *thank-you* page - just a simple thanks for reaching out message, with maybe a button to go back to the homepage or a "you can call us now" sort of option there. Whatever your style, when you're done, go down to the bottom of the page, open the RankMath box, go to Advanced, and set this page to *no-index*. This prevents accidental visitors from finding the page via search and skewing your data.

And that's it - we can monitor visits to the page in analytics. Again, for the best tracking data possible, integrating click events with Google Tag Manager would be preferable, even for this thank-you page. But today, we have a simple method for starting this process.

Google Business Profile (GBP)

Since we have a local component here, we definitely will be working with a GBP asset. If, for some crazy reason, this business doesn't have one yet, help them step through and create one. This is absolutely, 100% necessary for local.

I mentioned earlier that we utilize SEMRush Listing Management. So, with that, I'll give a few notes on "citations."

In SEMRush, it connects to the GBP profile, gives you a bunch of options in the dashboard for settings, and then goes on autopilot, cross-referencing this business in all of the major local listing sites (Apple Maps, Facebook, etc.), data aggregators (3rd party systems that provide local information to 3rd party apps), other top-level directories (Yellowpages, Yelp, etc), and then some seemingly random ones - but we let it do its thing and fix any issues the system flags. (One thing we don't do is set up a system like those cheap and well-known citation-building services that constantly dump random, low-level, nobody-ever-heard-of citations monthly on a company site. This is fruitless and pointless.)

We only need a base of major citations and a few minor ones, usually winding up with around 30 to 50 in SEMRush. That said, we will do one more thing. We'll head to Google and search for our target keywords related to the business we are working on and note all listing sites we find on pages 1 and 2.

We'll cross reference this with our list in SEMRush. If any are missing,, we will manually create them for the business. Since these sites are industry-relevant and are ranking pretty high, they're the next most important citations or listings we need to include for **this** business. Then, we're over all of that and moving on.

In the GBP profile itself, we want to ensure every function, bit of information, and asset we can use for this business is activated and correctly filled out. You want to include some light local keyword usage here but don't get carried away. And yes, direct keyword-match business names do work. But the right thing to do is to use the actual registered business name. I'll leave that at that…

Once you've done all you can do there, we have completed our baseline sweep.

Main Campaign

We have all of our ducks in rows, quacking in sequence, and now we can make our big moves and drive this thing to the top, increase those conversions, and watch this business grow online.

We have a couple of options here. We have our "low-hanging fruit" keywords. We have a list of pages that are doing well or almost doing well. You'll find some matches between those keywords and these pages if you're lucky. If so, start right there.

But what to do? Well, you've already optimized these pages and made all the moves you can with them, so now it's time to support and grow them with content.

The rhythm we'll use for this campaign is one Micro Funnel per week, making a Macro Funnel on a like subject by the end of the month. (Remember, a basic Micro Funnel is one main TFNA piece and two supporting articles.)

In this first month, we will hammer solely at our *next best bet* without venturing far from it (that's next month). We know we already have a conversion-focused main page for our target. We don't want to compete with it in search - sort of.

You see, Google is smart (sometimes) and the AI running the search results algo is pretty solid at understanding that specific user.

Google will serve the main landing for users ready to convert and just need that short and sweet path to get there.

For the same search, but someone who has been researching or is a historical "research" type of user, they'll get the TFNA piece on the same subject or one of the supporting articles if their search is skewed in that direction.

The problem is, right now, that the main page isn't ranking high enough for the first user. And we don't have the content for the second. The macro funnel approach here will solve this.

Doing our expansive deep dive into our first TFNA piece on this subject, we will cover all bases. We'll perform extensive research and start piecing together the framework to take that reader from research to consideration and conversion.

During that research, you should find questions on the subject being asked, popular content on a specific part of the subject, or something that deserves its own expanded explanation. This would fall under the umbrella of long-tail keyword targets.

This is when we add these to the keyword tracking system. Essentially, as we target them. We'll tag this in the tracker as "blog targets."

The TFNA piece would have that near-direct match keyword focus for our main target, just not an exact copy of what is said on the main site page we are also targeting.

In our first TFNA piece, we will find relevant areas in the content to insert deep links to the main site page we want to grow. Remember, TFNA has its own CTA integrated, so we will keep this as the target for conversion here, not the main page. What we are doing is creating multiple ways for multiple user types to convert.

For our supporting pieces, yes, they will share 2-way links with their TFNA mother, but they'll also deep link to that main page we are trying to grow. And now we have a mini network—a Micro Funnel—of like content, all integrated and targeting variations of both the subject and basic user types. But all of them share a connection with the main site page.

In this, we are telling Google that at the end of the day, we see the main landing as the most important thing in our framework. This is an important signal to send.

We'll repeat this process with further variations on the subject, aiming at the different user types we have found in our research, as discussed earlier in this book.

We are now accomplishing a bunch of things at once. We are developing a network of like information—each unique. Some pieces are expansive, and some are to the point. We're covering the subject in a way that no one else is at this moment. We will have more in-depth, up-to-date information about this than anyone else. And that is where we see near instant uplift.

With month 1 over, it's time to return to the keyword-tracking system.

Now, don't expect to see #1's all over the place. With consistent effort, give yourself at least 90 days from the day of implementation to evaluate placement or effect. But we will see movement here, or at least we should. This dictates whether we will forge down this path again this month or pivot to the next "low-hanging fruit."

Before deciding, run that site back through the Doman Overview Tool and SpyFu. Here, you may be surprised to find a slew of new keywords popping up on our radar. These are the direct effects of our content effort thus far.

Now is when you add more long-tail keywords to your tracking. We study what we see moving here, look at those that provide decent monthly tracking numbers, copy them to a list, and then upload them to our keyword tracker with our chosen tag.

With that set, you can easily identify how that content is doing over time. Let's say you see some uplift, but we're not #1 yet. In that case, Month 2 will have a little twist. We'll focus 3 of our Micro-Funnel efforts back on this same subject but then inject our next "low-hanging fruit" target into the mix with the 4th.

If they are similar (they should share similarities in most cases), we also create a larger web of internal links. Go back to your previous content and start adding links back and forth to these new ones.

At the end of that month, run the domain through the Doman Overview Tool and SpyFu again, looking for all the new things that are popping up. Add them to tracking, and keep going; moving from one target to the next as each becomes a winner.

The moment when you solidly pivot off a target is when you're in the top 3 in the SERPs. That's it, pivot to something else. But keep sprinkling a link from new content here and there back to these previous targets.

At about 90 days in, magic trick number two will start to bear fruit. Free organic links. They will come, and they will remain steady. With our massive content network, they will also go all over the place on the site - perfect! Since we always deep-linked back to the main website pages during our content creation process, we are now funneling link juice down to them.

And it is here, and as time passes, the cycle of content, links, incoming links, and growth - that we will have that final effect.

Our pages, regardless of the user type, where they are in the buying cycle, or what they are looking for (in our industry), our stuff is being served- To the right audience at the right time.

During all of this, we remain vigilant of repeating the cycle of studying GSC and GA4 data, constantly watching how we're growing in the keyword tracker, constantly finding new things to rank for, seeing the next best page to push, the next hot topic to hit, and always adjusting our active landing pages with fine-tuned CRO efforts.

Remember all those hard targets? This is where you start growing them.

Think of it this way: let's say the site wants to rank for "soccer balls." Can you imagine just trying to rank for that?

However, we have learned to figure out how people look for soccer balls, understand the topics the soccer world wants to read, and started crafting content around that.

To scientifically illustrate how this works, let's pretend to be Google for a minute:

You: "Hi. We sell soccer balls."

Google: "Nope, there are far better soccer ball sites out there. No, to you. Next!"

You: "Damn."

You: "Well, here is a content piece about regulation soccer balls."

Google: "Her3 iS a cOnteNt.. Blah, blah, pfft. Next!"

You: "Here's another about soccer ball dimensions and sizes for FIFA and youth leagues."

Google: "Well, you did break that down pretty good. Fine, page 3 for you."

You: "Here's an overview of how the materials used in soccer ball manufacturing can affect your game."

Google: "Damn, I didn't know that. Magical featured snippet for that one."

You: "Here's another detailing the evolution of the soccer ball.. if you're interested."

Google: "Fine."

You: "Here's why soccer is so popular across the globe, including its effects on local economies."

Google: "Damn, smooth move there."

You: "Here are the top-selling soccer balls of 2024."

Google: "That checks out."

You: "Here is our curated list of FIFA-approved soccer balls for sale."

Google: "Nice."

You: "We make custom soccer balls. Check it out."

Google: "Hmmm…"

Google: "Hello world! Check out this new soccer ball site! You can't miss them."

Or something like that.

E-Commerce

I didn't want to interrupt the flow of events that showed how all of this works, but I did mention I would talk about product optimization and things of that nature later in the book. This is later.

When we create content around an e-commerce category of products, such as a buyer's guide or a focused TFNA on the best ABC products for XYZ uses, we call out specific products and categories in each content piece. It is these products or product categories that you should focus on optimizing during that month. It's the best way for a small team or a DIY effort to manage this part of the process.

We work on sites with 100K SKUs, and it would be impossible for us to address them all quickly. Instead, as we move through content and target different things, we open each one up. We set that perfect meta title and description, but we also make sure the forward-facing, on-page side of things is optimized.

This includes the proper use of header tags and targeting, as well as creating original product descriptions.

In most e-commerce sites, almost everyone uses the **exact same** manufacturer-provided description for products. You have the opportunity to change this and stand out. Add your brand's voice to it. If you know a specific demographic tends to buy it, speak directly to them.

This is not as big of an effort as content creation, but it does take time and nuance. This is why we break down product optimization at this pace. We can maintain our high standards, get through the process over time, and know that the thing we just tried to grow in search through content - is just as optimized as the content we created around it. This is a winning cycle.

Local SEO

Do you know one thing Google loves, especially when it comes to GBP? It's relevance. I'm referring to the relevance of what is being targeted locally to that of the site itself. With your content effort and fine-tuned landing pages, you are constantly increasing your relevance and, frankly, your overall knowledge and authority in whatever niche you're in.

Imagine, for instance, Someone searching for a "service near me."

Google knows you're in town, but so are 100 others. However, Google looks at you differently. Because *you're* the authority on the subject—who also offers the solutions.

"Hey, searcher person, you're in luck. The absolute authority on the matter is right down the street—here is their GBP profile, and there they are at the top of regular results; they have an ad floating nearby, and... oh yeah, if you would like to explore the "people also ask" section, you'll find them there too."

Alongside all of that content you've been creating and sending out into the world, you have a never-ending supply of posts to share on GBP. All related, all on point, and all aiming at that ever-evolving conversion cycle you are in charge of.

It's a great feeling watching all of this work.

Now…

Get To Work

We truly appreciate you taking the time to see organic search marketing from our perspective. We promise if you give it some time and effort, you'll change your own world or that of your clients.

There is nothing left to do but to do it.

We'll find you in search!

Eric and Jack.

Series Info:
From Clicks to Conversions

From Clicks to Conversions: The Tactical Guide to Organic Search Marketing is the cornerstone of a comprehensive series designed to equip you with the knowledge and tools necessary for search marketing success. Recognizing the vastness of the field and the unique challenges faced by different types of marketers, we've intentionally structured this as a series rather than a single exhaustive volume. This approach allows you to tailor your learning and application process according to your specific needs and interests.

This book serves as the foundational guide, essential for all search marketers, regardless of their specific focus areas. We delve into the principles of organic search marketing, laying down the groundwork upon which all other strategies should be built.

Following this introductory guide, the series branches out into specialized field guides, each addressing a different facet of search marketing:

1. From Clicks to Conversions: The Field Guide to PPC This guide will take you through the intricacies of pay-per-click advertising, building upon the organic strategies covered in the main book to enhance your overall marketing approach.

2. From Clicks to Conversions: The Field Guide to Local Search Marketing – Tailored for businesses and marketers aiming to dominate local search results, this guide focuses on strategies to boost visibility and engagement within specific geographic areas.

3. From Clicks to Conversions: The Field Guide to Marketing a WordPress Site – Dive into the world of WordPress and learn how to leverage this popular platform to maximize your site's SEO and user engagement.

4. From Clicks to Conversions: The Field Guide to Marketing a Shopify Site – This guide is designed for e-commerce marketers focusing on Shopify, offering targeted strategies to enhance online store visibility and conversions.

By structuring the series in this way, we allow you to build a customized "course" that aligns with your marketing needs and goals. Start with *From Clicks to Conversions: The Tactical Guide to Organic Search Marketing* to grasp the foundational concepts and then select the field guides that best match the specific areas you wish to master. Together, these guides provide a comprehensive framework to navigate the search marketing landscape effectively.

About Your Authors

With a partnership that began in 2006, Eric Bonneman and Jack Bonneman's journey through the ever-evolving landscape of SEO has led them to develop groundbreaking strategies and techniques. Their combined expertise spans almost two decades, during which they have navigated through the highs and lows of search marketing trends, algorithm changes, and consumer behavior shifts. The techniques outlined here mirror the same proven process they employ at The King of Search.

Together, they have crafted *From Clicks to Conversions: The Tactical Guide to Organic Search Marketing*, encapsulating their years of experience, trials, and successes into a comprehensive guide. Their goal is simple yet profound: to provide unparalleled value and insight, sharing what they believe to be the most effective approach to search marketing in today's competitive environment.

Jack and Eric's approach is hands-on and grounded in real-world application. They believe in strategies that are not only theoretically sound but also practically viable. Their teachings are designed for anyone looking to make a significant impact in the digital space, from budding marketers to seasoned professionals.

With "From Clicks to Conversions," Jack and Eric invite you into their world, offering a glimpse into the strategies that have made them successful. They are not just sharing a methodology; they are offering a partnership in your journey towards search marketing excellence.

If you're ready to take your search marketing to the next level, explore more insights and resources at thekingofsearch .com/the-lab/, where they continue to pioneer authority-building, conversion-focused search marketing techniques.

www.ingramcontent.com/pod-product-compliance
Lightning Source LLC
Chambersburg PA
CBHW052132270326
41930CB00012B/2854